Sunset Bea[...]
Rerafu[...]

GW00370634

Right over bridge
Memesby...

TwinPack
Corfu

DES HANNIGAN

Canal Roller
[...] the Pigs

for Thus
meet rep

Des Hannigan is a writer
and photographer who has
written and contributed to
numerous travel-related books,
including AA guides to
Northern Europe, Andalucía,
Corfu, Rhodes and Pakistan.
He has longstanding
experience of Greece and of
the Greek islands especially.
He lives in the far west of
Cornwall, England.

Office 8.30 - 11
18.30 - 12

If you have any comments
or suggestions for this guide
you can contact the editor at
Twinpacks@theAA.com

AA Publishing
Find out more about AA Publishing
and the wide range of travel publications
and services the AA provides by visiting
our website at *www.theAA.com/bookshop*

Contents

life *5–12*

how to organise your time *13–22*

top 25 sights *23–48*

About this book

KEY TO SYMBOLS

✚ Grid reference to the Top 25 locator map

✉ Address

☎ Telephone number

🕐 Opening times

🍴 Restaurant or café on premises or near by

🚇 Nearest underground (tube) station

🚆 Nearest railway station

🚌 Nearest bus route

⛴ Nearest riverboat or ferry stop

♿ Facilities for visitors with disabilities

✋ Admission charge

↔ Other nearby places of interest

❓ Tours, lectures or special events

➤ Indicates the page where you will find a fuller description

ℹ Tourist information

TwinPack Corfu is divided into six sections to cover the six most important aspects of your visit to Corfu. It includes:

- The author's view of the island and its people
- Suggested walks and excursions
- The Top 25 sights to visit
- The best of the rest – aspects of the island that make it special
- Detailed listings of restaurants, hotels, shops and nightlife
- Practical information

In addition, easy-to-read side panels provide fascinating extra facts and snippets, highlights of places to visit and invaluable practical advice.

CROSS-REFERENCES

To help you make the most of your visit, cross-references, indicated by ➤ show you where to find additional information about a place or subject.

MAPS

The fold-out map in the wallet at the back of the book is a large-scale island map of Corfu.

The Top 25 locator maps found on the inside front and back covers of the book itself are for quick reference. They show the Top 25 sights, described on pages 24–48, which are clearly plotted by number (**1**–**25**, not page number) in alphabetical order.

PRICES

Where appropriate, an indication of the cost of an establishment is given by € signs. €€€ denotes higher prices, €€ denotes average prices, while € denotes lower prices.

CORFU
life

A Personal View

NAMES OLD AND NEW

The modern name of Corfu is said to derive from the Greek word *koryphai*, meaning 'summit' or 'twin peaks', a reference to the hills of the Old Fortress of Corfu Town. The older name for the island, Corcyra, or Kérkyra in modern Greek, is said to have been adopted in honour of the mythological nymph, Kérkura, who was abducted by Poseidon and brought to the island. In ancient times Corfu was known as Drepane, the word for 'sickle', a reference to the island's curved and elongated shape.

Corfu never fails to captivate. It has long been celebrated as the 'Garden Isle' of Greece and the rich tapestry of its swooping hills and deep valleys, clothed in acres of silver-leafed olive trees, their canopies pierced by tall stately cypresses, sets the tone; a perfect foil to the deep blue of the Ionian Sea and to the island's golden beaches.

The variety and quality of those beaches makes them irresistible and Corfu's many resorts are, understandably, the main attraction and main base for visitors, often from dawn to dusk. Beach life, night life, good food and wine in a smart restaurant or village taverna, fashionable shops and craft galleries – they all make up the high profile side of Holiday Corfu. But you should plan adventures too, by heading off into the hidden corners and magical byways of central Corfu, to the woods and mountains of the northeast and the more remote parts of the south and west coasts, to the timeless charm of mountain villages and to tiny bone-white churches perched on the edge of limestone cliffs.

Corfu is an all-year-round delight; its seasons are defined by the fragrance of orange blossom in winter, the vivid colours of wild flowers in spring and autumn, the hissing of cicadas in the summer's heat, the cool green shade of deep woodland, the musky perfume of pine trees. Unforgettable are early mornings on those summer beaches, when the freshness of the air mingles with the scent of the sea. Unforgettable too are those rosy summer evenings after a long languorous day of sun and sea.

Detail of the 'Madonna and Child', in the church of Ágios Spyrídonas, in the old town of Corfu

A fisherman drifts out on the waters of Corfu's New Port

ROMANTIC LEGEND

Corfu has been claimed as being the idyllic Scheria – 'like a shield laid on the misty sea', wrote Homer – the island of the Phaeacians, where the shipwrecked Odysseus was discovered by Nausicaa, daughter of King Alcinous. Several places on Corfu's coastline lay claim to be the spot where Odysseus was washed ashore, but the lovely bay at Érmones on the west coast is the favoured site.

HARVESTING OLIVES

Fallen olives were once painstakingly collected by hand. Now, nets are spread beneath the trees to make harvesting less labour intensive, but the work is still extremely hard. The Corfu olive, introduced by the Venetians, is used mainly to produce oil, rather than for eating as a fruit. Although some locals eat raw olives like grapes, visitors are advised not to; the experience is bitter.

Corfu is a fabled isle in every way; a modern holiday paradise, yet with an enduring heritage gleaned from its colourful and often turbulent past. Imprinted upon the island's landscape and life are the legacies of classical Greece, Byzantium, Rome and Venice, and those of later French and British influences, that made Corfu a crossroads of east and west without eroding its essential Greekness. You feel this extraordinary undertow of history most potently in the Campiello district, the oldest part of Corfu Town, amid a tangle of narrow alleyways hemmed in by the tall colour-washed façades of Venetian houses, whose crumbling walls, shapely mouldings and elegant balconies glow in the evening sun. Yet, these medieval streets, full of light and shade, give way seamlessly to the equally fascinating world of bustling shops, blaring traffic and voluble crowds in modern San Rocco Square. It is this happy mix of old and new Greece that underlines Corfu's enduring appeal.

If you bring to Corfu a sense of curiosity and discovery, along with well-founded expectations of a relaxing, sun-blessed holiday, then this loveliest of Greek islands will capture as well as captivate and will draw you back again and again.

Traditional costume on display in the History and Folklore Museum of central Corfu at Sinarádes

Corfu in Figures

GEOGRAPHY
- Position: Corfu is the most northerly of the Ionian Islands. The southeast coast lies about 10km from mainland Greece, the northeast about 2km from Albania.
- Area: 592sq km.
- Highest point: Mount Pandokrator, at 906m.
- Length, north to south: 60km.
- Width, east to west: 4km to 30km. Length of coastline: 217km.
- Population: 110,000 approximately, of which about 35,000 live in Corfu Town.

CLIMATE
- Corfu has a higher average rainfall than the rest of Greece. The highest monthly rainfall is in December, with 240mm. The summer months are almost entirely dry.
- Average daily sunshine, May–September: 10 hours.
- Average temperature, July–August: 32°C.
- Average temperature, December–January: 15°C.

ECONOMIC FACTORS
- About 65 per cent of Corfu's land is under cultivation. Of this, 55 per cent is devoted to olive trees, of which there are an estimated 3.5 million. The rest of the cultivated area is used for vineyards, citrus fruit, vegetables and grazing.
- About one million tourists visit Corfu annually and an estimated third of Corfu's working population is involved in tourism and its related industries.

The slopes of Mount Pandokrator, viewed from the vantage point of Ipsos beach

People of Corfu

St Spyrídon

St Spyrídon (AD 270–c348) is the patron saint of Corfu and a focus of strong devotion on the island where he is known simply as 'The Saint'. Spyrídon was a Cypriot bishop, said to have performed numerous miracles. During the 7th century, the saint's revered remains were transferred from Cyprus to Constantinople, but, on the fall of the city in 1453, his body was brought, eventually, to Corfu by an itinerant priest. The remains lie in the Church of St Spyrídon (▶ 25). St Spyrídon is associated with several miraculous events which saved the island from plague, famine and Turkish siege and these are celebrated with solemn, but colourful, processions in which his remains are carried through Corfu Town.

Ioannis Kapodistrias (John Capodistrias)

Count John Capodistrias (1776–1831) was a celebrated Corfiot who, in 1827, became the first President of Independent Greece. In 1831 his career was cut short, however, when he was assassinated at Náfplio in the Peloponnese by violent critics of his political programme.

Born in Corfu in 1776, Capodistrias practised as a doctor, and then entered island politics. During the French occupation of Corfu he left the island and joined the Russian foreign service. In 1822 he retired and devoted himself to the cause of Greek independence.

Capodistrias is buried in Moní Platytéras (the Monastery of Platitéra) in Corfu Town. A small museum in Evropoúli, to the west of the town, celebrates his life.

Nicholas Mantzaros

Corfu has produced internationally recognised composers such as Spiros Samaras (1861–1917), but probably the most famous Corfiot musical celebrity is Nicholas Chalikiopoulos Mantzaros (1795–1872), who composed the Greek national anthem as an accompaniment to the poem *A Hymn to Freedom*, written by the celebrated poet Dionysios Solomos. Mantzaros devoted much of his later life to teaching and, at times, to financing young Corfiot students.

ISLAND TALENT

Corfu-based painters of Cretan origin, such as Emmanuel Tzanes (1610–90) and Michael Damaskinos (1530–92), have produced some of the finest icon paintings of Greece. Modern Corfiot painters include Nikos Venturas (1899–1990) and Papa Aglaia (1904–84). Corfu has also inspired several famous British exiles, including the painter and writer Edward Lear (1812–88) and the writers Gerald and Lawrence Durrell.

The silver sarcophagus containing the remains of the 4th-century St Spyrídon

A Chronology

8000 BC	Corfu becomes an island when sea levels rise at the end of the ice ages.
6000 BC	The island is settled by neolithic hunter-gatherers.
3000–1000 BC	Several Bronze Age settlements are established throughout Corfu.
750 BC	Eretrians colonise the Kanóni Peninsula. They may have named their settlement Corcyra (Kérkyra) after the mythological goddess Kérkura.
734 BC	Political refugees from Corinth supplant the Eretrians and establish a thriving colony.
303 BC–229 BC	Corcyra is invaded at various times by adventurers from Syracuse, by later Macedonian kings, and finally by Illyrian pirates, who prey on Roman ships.
229 BC	Corcyra becomes a Roman colony, the first in Greece.
AD 70	Christian influence is brought to the island by saints Jason and Sosipater (▶ 14).
395	Corcyra comes under the control of the Byzantine Empire.
550	The island is devastated by Goth invaders. The promontory, where the Old Fortress now stands, becomes the nucleus of a fortified town. The name Corfu, from the Greek word *koryphai*, meaning 'summit' or 'twin peaks', first emerges.
1080	Corfu is taken over by the Norman Robert Guiscard, King of Sicily. In 1149 Corfu is recaptured by the Byzantine Emperor Manuel Comnenus.
1214	Michael I, Despot of Epirus, takes over Corfu. Renewed Byzantine influence underpins the official position of the Greek Church.

1267	The Neapolitan House of Anjou gains control of Corfu.
1386	Corfu offers allegiance to Venetians, who rule the island for four centuries. Orthodox religion and Greek customs and culture survive.
1456	The body of St Spyrídon is brought to Corfu from Constantinople.
1537	First major siege by the Turks, who ravage the island but fail to take the Old Fortress and Angelókastro. They withdraw with about 15,000 prisoners.
1565	Venetians order the uprooting of vineyards and a widespread planting of olive trees, a scheme finally achieved only by offering farmers handsome payment for every 100 trees planted.
1570s	Building of the New Fortress.
1716	Second major Turkish siege is repulsed.
1797	Corfu and the other Ionian Islands are captured by the French.
1814	Corfu becomes part of the United States of the Ionian Islands under British Protection.
1864	On 21 May, Corfu becomes part of united Greece, whose first Governor is the Corfu-born politician Ioannis Kapodistrias (John Capodistrias).
1940–44	Corfu Town bombed by the Italians, and later by the Germans.
1960s	Development of mass tourism.
1994	Corfu hosts the EC summit.
2002	Greece adopts the euro as its currency.
2004	Greece host the Olympic Games.

Best of Corfu

If you only have a short time to visit Corfu, or would like to get a complete picture of the island, here are the essentials:

- Explore Corfu Town (➤ 29). Absorb the hectic buzz of modern San Rocco Square, then stroll northeast along Georgiou Theotoki and Voulgareos streets, with side steps into the shaded alleyways of the Old Town, before bursting out into the sunshine and open space of the Spianáda (Esplanade, (➤ 48).
- Walk along a track through peaceful olive groves, on the hills, or above the sea.
- Eat at a top-quality village or beach taverna where good Greek food is served, such as Stamatis at Virós, or Toula's at Agni. Be talk-ative, be lively. Indulge yourself.
- Take a boat trip round the coast, or out to the Diapondía Islands, or south to Paxoí (Paxos). A leisurely view from the sea increases familiarity with Corfu.
- Visit one of Corfu's inland villages, such as Doukádes, Ágios Mattheos, Lefkímmi or Sinarádes. Wander freely, but discreetly, into authentic Corfu.
- Swim…and swim again…and again…and again…

The rococo-style belfry of the church of Zoodochos Pighi or the Source of Life

- Visit at least some of Corfu Town's historic, religious and cultural sites.
- Live a little nightlife, depending on your taste. Try the sound and light shows in the Old Citadel, a Greek evening in a taverna, a blitz of sound at any of the resort clubs or on the disco strip on Eth Antistasseos on the coast road to the northwest of Corfu Town.
- Visit Paleokastritsa for its astonishing coastal and mountain landscape, its small but delightful beaches, its absorbing monastery, and the drama of the nearby hilltop ruin of Angelókastro.
- Climb Mount Pandokrator or Mount Ágios Mattheos, but go as early in the day as possible.

CORFU
how to organise your time

13

A Walk into the Past

INFORMATION

Distance 5km
Time 1.5 hours
Start point Maitland Rotunda
End point San Rocco Square
Lunch Cafés and tavernas
✉ Mitr Athanassiou (€)

The Maitland Rotunda (1816) at the south of the Spianáda (Esplanade)

Many historic monuments are passed on this walk through the southern part of Corfu Town.

Start at the Peristýlio Maitland (Maitland Rotunda, ➤ 48). Continue south on Dimokratias, alongside the sea, for 1.7km to reach the small harbour at Anemomylos. Here, on the seaward point, beyond the Nautilus Café, is a restored windmill. Pass the café and bear round right along the edge of the sea until opposite the Hotel Mon Repos. Cross the road, with care, then go down the lane to the left of the hotel. Pass Ágios Iásonas kai Sosipátros (the Byzantine Church of St Jason and St Sosipater) on the left.

Turn first right just past the church. Reach a tree-shaded walkway (toilets) and turn left. At a road junction cross left, with care, and follow the continuation walkway to reach Oveliskos Ntalklas (the Douglas Obelisk). Cross left to the British Consulate.

The obelisk commemorates General Sir Howard Douglas, the 4th British High Commissioner, an able administrator.

Go up the street to the left of the consulate. At a junction go straight across and past railings to reach Stíli tou Menekráti (the Tomb of Menekrates).

This 6th-century cenotaph celebrates Menekrates, a representative of ancient Corcyra.

Continue along Kyprou (Cyprus) Street for about 100m, then go sharp right on to a road rising through trees. Continue until you reach a T-junction by the walls of Corfu Prison. Turn left and follow the walls round past the prison's main gate. Bear left, and then right down Kolokotroni Street to Angliká Nekrotafeío (the British Cemetery). Continue on to a busy junction with Mitropolitou Methodiou. Turn right and continue to San Rocco Square.

A Walk to a Spectacular View

The route leads from a Corfiot mountain village through olive groves to a tiny chapel.

Start at the square in Doukádes (➤ 54). The village probably originated during a period of devastating pirate raids on Corfu's coastal communities when people retreated to the more remote interior.

Continue along the main street for 30m, then go up right between stone steps and a telegraph pole. Climb to the old church with its red-domed apse. Keep to the right of the church and go up the stepped path.

Note the Venetian mansion on the right, complete with Italian name-plate on the wall.

When the path meets a roughly surfaced road, go right. Follow the road as it twists and turns uphill through olive groves. Leave the road where it bends sharply right and follow the rough track ahead crossing sections of ribbed concrete. Soon the track turns west and levels off.

This is typical olive-growing country, remote and with a variety of wild flowers in spring.

At a junction turn left. Go down through olive trees, then climb uphill. After a stony section the track ends at a clearing. At the far side of this go down a narrow, rocky path to reach the tiny Chapel of St Simeon.

The chapel stands at the very edge of sheer cliffs. Take great care, of children especially, when close to the unprotected edge. There are spectacular views down to the Paleokastritsa road, south to the villages of Gardeládes and Liapádes, and to Paleokastritsa itself.

Retrace your steps along the same route back to Doukádes.

INFORMATION

Distance 4km
Time 2 hours
Start end/point Doukádes
  If using your own transport, approach from the Paleokastritsa road. Go through the village to its northern end to a little car park down a slip road on the left. Walk back uphill to the village square
🚌 Green bus from Avramiou Street, Corfu Town–Paleokastritsa
Lunch Choice of tavernas in Doukádes (€)

The finely carved doorway to the village church in Doukádes

15

A Walk on the Northeast Coast

The route leads from the pleasant, undeveloped beach at Avláki, first by road, past dense olive groves, and then through a delightful wooded area where tracks take you back down to the coast and a smaller beach, before returning to Avláki.

Start at the east end of Avláki Beach. Follow the road east and uphill for about 1km, and then, where the road bends sharply right and uphill, go left and off the road. Ignore a track running up right. Instead pick your way past dumped rubble and follow a rough path that leads past a deep hole on the right. The path becomes more distinct as it climbs a steep slope. At the top of the slope, where there is a wire fence on the right, go sharply left and follow a good track, downhill at first, then uphill.

The track leads through a delightful area of trees and bushes where the ground is brilliant with wild-flowers in spring. Look out for cyclamen, valerian, anemones and in autumn such scented herbs as thyme, sage and oregano. Spring is a good time for bird-watching, and in the dense, moist groves around Avláki migrant birds to look out for include nightingale, spotted flycatcher, black-headed bunting and warbler

Dappled shade below the boughs of mature olive trees makes for ideal walking

At a junction with a broad track go left. (Alternatively, a right turn will lead you back to the road where another right turn leads to Avláki Beach.) At the next junction turn right and follow a track towards the sea. At a junction in a grassy dip head down left to a small beach. At the left end of the beach (looking out to sea) seek out the hidden start to a good path that leads through dense woodland to emerge at Avláki Beach.

A Drive Around Northeast Corfu

This is a route of dramatic contrasts, following Corfu's scenic northeast coast and returning through the mountains.

Start at the Old Port in Corfu Town. Drive west from Old Port along Xenofondos Stratigou and Eth Antistasseos. Continue along the coast road for 3km to a big junction. Go right, and after 10km, at Tzavros, turn off right, signposted Dassiá. Pass through Dassiá (▶ 52), Ýpsos (Ipsos) and Barmbáti (Barbati ▶ 52). Pass through Nisáki (Nisaki) and 5km further on reach the turn off for Kalámi (▶ 32).

Parking is limited at Kalámi, but there is a large lay-by on the main road just before the turn off. From here it is just under 1km to Kalámi and its neighbour, Kouloúra (▶ 54).

Continue along main road to Kassiópi (▶ 72) and on to Acharávi (Ahravi, ▶ 50). Halfway through Acharávi's wide main street, pass a walled round-about with an old waterpump at its centre. About 150m further on, look out for a signpost pointing left to Epískepsi and Ágios Panteleímon. Turn left on to a narrow road. Continue steeply and through many bends (you will need to watch out for occassional pot-holes). In 5km, you will reach Epískepsi.

Epískepsi is a traditional mountain village at the heart of olive-growing country.

Continue for 9km to reach Sgourádes. (Watch out for children on narrow bends through the village.) After 10km reach a junction with a road going off left, signposted Petáleia and Strinýlas (Strinilas). This road leads in about 7km to Mount Pandokrator. Divert if desired.

On the main route, continue downhill to Spartýlas. In the 4km descent to the coast road there are 25 hair-raising hairpins with stunning views all the way down: concentrate. At the coast road, turn right and return to Corfu Town through Ýpsos (Ipsos).

INFORMATION

Distance 80km (100km if Mount Pandokrator is included)
Time 6 hours, with stops; 7–8 hours if Mount Pandokrator is included
Start/end point Corfu Town
Lunch Pepes (€€) ✉ Kalámi
☎ (26630) 91180

A Drive Around the Northwest

A drive to the famous resort of Paleokastritsa, followed by a climb over the mountains to Sidári (► 46). The return to Corfu Town is via the scenic Troumbetas Pass.

INFORMATION

Distance 105km
Time 6–7 hours, with stops
Start end/point Old Port, Corfu Town
Lunch Golden Fox (€€)
✉ Lákones

Start at the Old Port in Corfu Town. Drive west along the coast road for 3km to a big junction, and turn right. Follow signs for Paleokastritsa.

Visit Paleokastritsa (► 42).

Return from Paleokastritsa, and at the junction by the Paleo Club, turn sharp left uphill, signposted Lákones. Climb through a succession of hairpin bends to Lákones.

The route passes several restaurants with spectacular views from their roadside terraces.

Viewed from high on the wooded hillside, the coastline around the celebrated beauty spot of Paleokastritsa

Reach Makrádes. (Go left through Kríni to visit the hilltop fortress ruin of Angelókastro, ► 27.) On the main route, leave Makrádes, keeping right at junctions. Pass through Vístonas and continue for 7km to Troumbetas.

Turn left here and descend through several big hairpins, then, at a junction on a right-hand bend, go left, signposted Sidári and Aríllas. Continue to a big junction and keep ahead into Sidári.

Sidári has enough beach attractions, cafés, tavernas and shops to keep everyone happy.

Return to the big junction and go left. At the entrance to Róda, turn right at a junction, signposted Kérkyra (Corfu Town). Keep right at the next junction. Follow the main road for about 12km, keeping left at big junctions and climbing through S-bends to reach Troumbetas. Continue downhill through S-bends to the junction with the Paleokastritsa road. Turn left for Corfu Town.

A Drive Around South Corfu

This drive passes the Achilleion then continues south through Benítses and Boúkaris before returning along a winding mountain road (minor roads may have pot-holes).

Start at the Old Port in Corfu Town. Drive west from the Old Port along Xenofondos Stratigou and Eth Antistasseos. Continue along the coast road for 3km to a big junction. Take the left turn, signposted Lefkímmi. Follow signs for Lefkímmi and Achilleío (Ahillio). In about 4km, at the busy Vrioni junction, keep right, signposted Achilleío. Follow Achilleío signs to reach Gastoúri and then the Achilleion (▶ 24) itself which is worth visiting.

Continue from the Achilleion and descend steeply through numerous bends to the coast road. Turn right and continue to Benítses.

Old Benítses (▶ 28), at the northern entrance to the resort, is a charming place to explore.

Continue south to Moraïtika. At the junction beyond the resort, where the main road bends sharply right, go straight across. In about 500m, at a T-junction, take the left turn, signposted Messongí Beach and Boukari Beach. At the next T-junction by the supermarket, turn right and follow a narrow coastal road for 4km to Boúkaris. Turn sharp right and uphill between tavernas. Continue to Kouspádes. Beyond the village, keep right at the next junction, signed Petrití, then go downhill. At the next junction, on a right-hand bend, keep right and continue to Neohoraki. Climb steeply to reach a T-junction at Argyrádes (worth lingering in). Turn right.

Continue north and, after 9km, cross a bridge. At a junction on a sharp right-hand bend, signposted Corfu and Benítses to the right, go straight across on to a narrow road. Continue to Ágios Déka. Drive very carefully through the village, then descend through several steep bends. At a T-junction, go right, signposted Kérkyra, and follow signs the town.

INFORMATION

Distance 60km
Time 4–5 hours, with stops at the Achilleion and Benítses included
Start/end point Corfu Town
Lunch Boúkari Beach taverna (€–€€)
✉ Boúkaris

19

Finding Peace & Quiet

The lushness of Corfu's famous olive groves is a pleasing contrast to the cobalt blue of the Mediterranean. It is this wealth of woodland that provides the island's havens of peace and quiet, areas where the beach-weary visitor can explore and find cool shade from the sun. On the higher ground of the mountains, and along the undeveloped coast, there are other opportunities to escape from the crowds.

TOWNS AND VILLAGES

Peace and quiet is not only a rural luxury. In busy, bustling Corfu Town there are oases of calm, such as the larger Orthodox churches that are open to the public, the various museums, and the British Cemetery. And, in mountain villages, a more relaxed, more serene attitude is the norm.

WALKING*

The best walking areas are on the more remote northeast and west coasts, and on the high ground of Mount Pandokrator, Mount Ágios Matthéos and Mount Ágios Déka. However, by walking inland through olive groves, peace and quiet can also be found within a few metres of busy resorts. Of interest to any walking enthusiast is the Corfu Trail, a 200km fully-marked walk crossing the whole island. The route meanders through diverse landscapes, linking beauty spots, beaches, picturesque villages, monuments and monasteries. The entire walk can be done in 8 to 12 days, alternatively you can pick out sections, as detailed in the guide book (➤ 21) or on the website (www.corfutrail.com).

A deserted sunny street in the village of Afiónas

CYCLING

Hire bikes can be used for the multitude of off-road tracks on the island. The least hilly areas are in the south, round Límni Korissión and Lefkímmi, in the western Rópa Valley area, and in the north, round coastal Sidári, Róda and Acharávi. But, anywhere on the island, you

The view towards Pélekas from Kaiser Wilhelm's telescope

should be prepared for rough surfaces, pot-holes and for some steep climbs.

WILDLIFE

Corfu has over 400 species of wild plant, most of which bloom during spring and early summer, while autumn sees another flowering of certain species. Masses of daisies appear early, followed by pink geraniums, marigolds, irises, poppies and grape hyacinths, among many others. On the higher ground of the mountains, blue anemones and bell-headed fritillaries light up the landscape, while the limestone rocks are clothed in purple-pink soapwort. Over 30 species of orchid grow on Corfu, including the bee orchid, Jersey orchid, man orchid, tongue orchid and monkey orchid.

Migrant birds pass through Corfu in vast numbers in spring and autumn. Species include warblers, flycatchers, whitethroats and the jackdaw-sized blue roller. Summer residents include swallows, sand martins and bee-eaters.

A cocktail of fragrances from Corfu's flowers and shrubs attracts numerous butterflies, such as the yellow-orange cleopatra, the chocolate-brown Camberwell beauty and the long-tailed blue.

Reptiles include the harmless four-lined snake, which can grow to over a metre in length. Two venomous species are the Lataste's, or horn viper, recognised by its distinctive horned nose, and the Montpellier snake, grey, brown or olive in colour and with prominent ridges over the eyes. Such snakes will instinctively avoid you. The most avid 'biters' on Corfu are midsummer horse-flies.

*A reprint of the excellent *Green Map* of Corfu that details roads, dirt tracks and trails is underway; ask at bookshops. Recommended guides are *The Second Book of Corfu Walks: The Road to Old Corfu*, *In the Footsteps of Lawrence Durrell and Gerald Durrell* and *The Companion Guide to the Corfu Trail*, all by Hilary Whitton Paipeti.

The tree-lined horse-shoe bay of Kouloúra

21

What's On

JANUARY	*New Year's Day* (1 Jan). *Epiphany* (6 Jan): Religious ceremonies held.
FEBRUARY/MARCH	*Pre-Lenten Carnival*: Sunday before Lent there is a big carnival procession in Corfu Town. *Clean Monday, Kathari Deftera*: Monday after Carnival Sunday. Picnics and kite flying. *8 March*: St Theodora's Day. The saint's remains are carried around Corfu Town.
APRIL	*Easter (movable)*: The most important celebration of the Greek year. Religious services are held during the preceding Holy Week. *Palm Sunday*: The remains of St Spyrídon are carried in procession through Corfu Town. *Good Friday*: Church processions. *Easter Saturday*: Procession from Church of St Spyrídon. Pot-throwing custom. Candle-lit ceremony of the Resurrection on the Esplanade. Fireworks display. *Easter Sunday*: Resurrection parades from churches. Countless fairs throughout the island.
MAY	*1 May*: National holiday festival at Róda and on Mount Ágios Déka. *4 May*: Feast of St Thomas festivals. *8 May*: Festival at Kassiópi. *21 May*: Ionian Day. Local holiday.
JUNE	*Pentecost Sunday*: Festival at Lákones. *Whit Monday*: Festivals at Kondókali, Stavros and Argirádes, among others. *29 June*: Major festival celebrating St Gáïos at Gáïos on Paxos.
JULY	*8 July*: St Prokopios's Day. Festival at Lefkímmi. *26 July*: St Paraskevi's Day. Festivals at Avliótes, Ágios Matthéos, Benítses, Ipsos, Kinopiastes.
AUGUST	*6 August*: Saviour's Day. During the preceding week there are pilgrimages to the summit of Mount Pandokrator. *11 August*: St Spyrídon's Day. Procession of casket holding the saint's remains through Corfu Town. *15 August*: Assumption of the Virgin. Festivals at Platitéra Monastery and at numerous villages.

CORFU'S
top 25 sights

The sights are shown on the maps on the inside front cover and inside back cover, numbered **1**–**25** alphabetically

Achilleío (Ahillio)

INFORMATION

➕ C2

✉️ Gastoúri village.
Signposted from Corfu
Town and from the coast
road north of Benítses

☎ (26610) 56245

🕐 Daily Jun–Aug 8–7;
Sep–May 9–3.30

🍽 Cafés (€€) near entrance

🚌 Blue bus 10 from San
Rocco Square, Corfu
Town

♿ Few

💲 Expensive

↔️ Benítses (▶ 28)

❓ Roadside parking only;
very crowded during Jul
& Aug

Corfu's famous Achilleion Palace is a delightful expression of 19th-century classicism and indulgence, set within beautiful surroundings.

The Achilleion, a fascinating relic of 19th-century grand design and occasionally dubious taste, stands on tree-clad heights above the east coast resort of Benítses, adjacent to the village of Gastoúri. It was conceived by the Empress Elizabeth of Austria as a tribute to her spiritual hero Achilles, and the result is a splendid confection of colonnades and stucco work based on the classical elegance of Pompeii, the whole crowded with statues, paintings and 19th-century furnishings.

Six years after the palace was completed in 1892, the Empress was killed by an assassin on the quayside of Lake Geneva. In 1908 the palace was bought by Kaiser Wilhelm II, who added his own grandiose touches before leaving Corfu in 1914 for more pressing engagements – he never returned. Eventually taken over by the Greek state, the Achilleion lay unused until it was converted into a casino in 1963. Today, the casino is part of the Corfu Holiday Palace.

On view is the ornately decorated entrance hall, the Empress's chapel, and ground-floor reception rooms containing furnishings and memorabilia of the Empress and the Kaiser. In the terraced gardens, beneath the shade of cypresses and palm trees, are numerous statues including the Empress's favourite, the sentimental 'Dying Achilles', and a contribution from the Kaiser, an outrageously monumental 'Achilles Triumphant'.

The highly romanticised marble statue of 'Dying Achilles'

Ágios Spyrídonas

Ágios Spyrídonas is the most famous church in Corfu. Built in 1590 to house the sacred relics of St Spyrídon, it is a place of pilgrimage to this day.

The tall, red-domed bell-tower of Ágios Spyrídonas, reminiscent of the tower of San Giorgio dei Greci in Venice, is a landmark of central Corfu Town. Plain outside walls hide a lavish interior: there is a superb iconostasis (a screen of white Cycladian marble); silver thuribles and candelabra crowd the basilica; and a wealth of paintings and icons decorate the walls.

In spite of the steady procession of the faithful – and the merely curious – which passes across the pink-and-white flagstones and through the doors to either side, there is a subdued atmosphere inside the church. Candles still flicker in the gloom 'like yellow crocuses', as vividly described by Gerald Durrell in his reminiscences of a Corfu childhood. Young and old, the plain and the fashionable pay homage to St Spyrídon.

The real focus of the church, however, is the ornate casket containing the mummified remains of the saint. These are exposed annually on 12 December (St Spyrídon's Day), at Easter, and on 11 August. The saint's feet are clad in embroidered slippers, which devotees claim become worn because of Spyrídon's frequent night-time wanderings round the Old Town. The casket, silver-coated and bearing 12 enamel medallions, is situated to the right of the altar, within a separate chapel, beneath lamps and votive offerings from which dangle tiny silver ships and other motifs. Only a few steps take you from the dazzling sunshine of the outside world into this intense focus of Greek Orthodoxy.

INFORMATION

- 🕂 B2
- ✉ Ayiou Spiridonas Street, Corfu Town. Can also be reached from Plateía Iroon Kypriakou Agonos, known also as St Spyrídon's Square
- 🕐 Daily 9–2. Casual visits during services are best avoided
- 🍴 Café Plakada (€€) in St Spyrídon's Square
- ♿ Good (best access is from Ayiou Spiridonas Street)
- 💷 Free, donations welcome
- ❓ Sober clothing should be worn

A fresco depicting the patron saint of Corfu, St Spyrídon

(handwritten) tres, stopped off, very minimessy beach

Ágios Stefanos (Northeast)

Fishing village Ágios Stéfanos has kept its traditional character while adapting gracefully to its other role as a resort.

INFORMATION

🕂 B3

✉ 35km north of Corfu Town on northeast coast. A 3km lane leads to the village from Siniés on the main coast road

🍴 Several tavernas (€€)

🚌 Green bus from Avramiou Street, Corfu Town

🚢 Kerasiá can be reached from Kassiópi and other resorts by boat

🔁 Kassiópi (► 34)

❓ Limited parking

An 18th-century chapel in the resort of Ágios Stéfanos

Set within the arms of a quiet bay beneath tree-covered slopes, it is reached down a road which winds through olive groves, then descends through steep bends to the coast. White-walled buildings lie behind the beach, wooden jetties project into the bay, and fishing boats come and go. Early and late in the day, it feels as if the way of life that has flourished here for generations has hardly changed at all. To the east, across the narrow waters of the Corfu Channel, lies Albania, here at its closest point to Corfu. The beaches become crowded in summer when excursion boats bring day visitors from nearby Kassiópi and Kalámi. There are excursions in turn from Ágios Stéfanos, and boats can be hired for exploring the coast and coves to either side. Beach equipment can be hired too, and some watersports are available.

Tracks and paths lead north to the isolated beach at Avláki (► 16). The road south continues through well-tended, wooded countryside criss-crossed with immaculate limestone walls. After about 1.5km it ends at the very long beach of Kerasiá. Although this is an undeveloped area – apart from a single taverna and some villas – Paralía Kerasiás (Kerasiá Beach) is very popular with day visitors who arrive in large numbers by excursion boat. By evening the beach regains a sense of pleasant isolation, though it forfeits the sun.

Angelókastro

The 12th-century ruin of the Byzantine fortress of Angelókastro occupies a spectacular rocky hill top on the west coast.

Angelókastro is one of the finest historic sites on Corfu. Fortified in the 12th century, it may later have been named after the Byzantine family of Angeloi Komneni, which ruled Corfu during the 11th and 12th centuries. The fortress played a key role in the successful defence of the island for hundreds of years, as from it a watch could be kept on the vulnerable west coast and signals exchanged with Corfu Town. Angelókastro's greatest test came when several thousand islanders withstood sieges by Turkish invaders in 1537, 1571 and 1716. When Venetian rule ended in 1797, Angelókastro lost its strategic relevance and began its long decline. During French control of the island, it was used as a maritime lookout and semaphore station, but military responsibility ended during the British Protectorate and the fortress was abandoned.

The ruins of the fortress stand on top of a rocky pinnacle whose seaward cliffs drop 300m into the sea. During the spring, wild roses and orchids speckle the steep slopes. Cobbled steps wind steeply from a convenient car park to a narrow entrance into the inner keep, above which is the upper keep, crowned by the tiny Church of the Archangels Michael and Gabriel, another possible source of Angelókastro's name. In front of the church are seven grave moulds cut into the rock.

Just east of the summit, and at a lower level, are the remains of underground water cisterns. In the lower keep, on the far left of the entrance, is a remarkable hermitage – a rocky cave that was converted into a chapel to St Kyriaki in the late 18th century. Wall-paintings of the Virgin and Christ survive.

INFORMATION

- ✚ A1
- ✉ Kríni. Just west of Makrádes (follow the signs) and 28km from Corfu Town
- 🕐 Daily May–Sep 8.30–3
- 🍴 Castelo St Angelo Taverna (€€) beside car park
- 🚌 Green bus from Avramiou Street, Corfu Town–Makrádes, then 2.5km walk
- ♿ None
- 💶 Cheap
- ↔ Paleokastritsa (▶ 42)
- ❓ Take care near the unprotected cliff edges

27

Benítses

There are two Benítses: brash resort and traditional Greek village. Old Benítses is an absolute delight while the resort is popular with clubbers.

INFORMATION

- ✚ C2
- ✉ 13km south of Corfu Town on main road
- 🍴 Paxinos Taverna (€€), just inside the Old Village
- 🚌 Blue bus 6, from San Rocco Square, Corfu Town–Pérama–Benítses
- 🚢 Excursion boats
- ♿ Beach beside road
- ↔ The Achilleion (➤ 24)
- ❓ Toilets at village square. Car parking at north and south ends of resort

In traditional Benítses, fishing caiques, laden with brightly coloured nets and floats, lie with their bows towards the little harbour quays. Across the main road from the harbour is the village square with its mix of Venetian buildings and two-storeyed houses, busy little cafés and tavernas. A short distance north from the square, a narrow alleyway (signposted 'Roman Baths') leads between seafront houses, to a lemon grove and the small but impressive ruins of the bathhouse of a Roman villa. The old village also extends inland along a narrow lane (signposted) to the right of a supermarket. Amid the citrus trees and bougainvillaea is a fine old church with a well-head in its courtyard. The remarkable Corfu Shell Museum (daily 10–8) at the northern entrance to Benítses is worth a visit. It is one of the biggest and best-curated collections of shells from worldwide locations.

Pavement restaurant in Benítses

Resort Benítses lies south of the old village, beyond the tiny roadside Church of St Dimitrious with its single bell-tower and tiled roof. The resort is the hub of a busy social whirl during the summer, especially for young North Europeans seeking Mediterranean sun and fast food and fast music. The resort's reputation for all-night fun and games has mellowed in recent years, although the clubs and bars are still lively. The beach is a grudgingly narrow shingle strip with the busy main road alongside. All types of watersport are available, and you can hire sunbeds for pavement grilling if the beach is impossibly crowded.

Campiello

Corfu Town's old quarter lies behind the seafront between the Old and New Fortresses and is known as Campiello.

INFORMATION

🔠 B2

🍴 Numerous cafés, tavernas and restaurants throughout the Old Town

♿ None. Steps link a number of alleyways and streets

Venetian is the emphatic style of Campiello's buildings and its fascinating maze of narrow streets, the *kandounia*, which spreads between the main thoroughfares; lanes are often linked by stone stairways (*skalinades*), and by vaulted passageways. The original buildings of the medieval town, which developed on the cramped peninsula as a domestic adjunct to the Old Fortress, eventually replacing it as the administrative centre of the island, are long gone. Here, the Venetians built grand Renaissance houses three or four storeys high, which were added to in later centuries to accommodate a growing population whose members were reluctant to move outside the town walls.

Venetian motifs survive on the sometimes crumbling façades of these wonderful old buildings and on the doorcases, or *portonia*, with their distinctive mouldings. Throughout the day the sun weaves an intricate pattern of shifting light on the walls and turns them to burnished gold in the evening. In the narrow, sun-dappled canyons of Campiello, lines of washing hang like banners between the upper windows, and the mottled walls rise cliff-like past railed balconies and stone pediments to a final blue ribbon of sky. Underfoot the ground is smoothly paved, and intriguing courtyards, terraced gardens, ancient churches and shrines appear round every other corner. There are neighbourhood shops, cafés, tavernas, bars and workplaces where Corfiots busy themselves with trade and craft. In the mellow evenings, you may catch the sound of musicians hard at work practising in the club rooms of the town's four brass bands.

Érmones

INFORMATION

- ✚ B1
- ✉ 17km from Corfu Town on west coast. Reached from Rópa Valley, through Vátos
- 🍴 Nausika Restaurant Bar (€–€€)
- 🚌 Green bus from Avramiou Street, Corfu Town–Vátos
- 🚢 Excursion boats to and from other resorts
- ↔ Glyfáda (► 52–53)
- ℹ Limited parking above beach

The funicular railway starts its descent from the Érmones Beach Hotel

Picturesque Érmones Bay claims to be the place where Homer's Odysseus was washed ashore after his voyage from Calypso's isle.

Here Odysseus was discovered by the beautiful Nausicaa, daughter of Alcinous, King of the Phaeacians – the legendary inhabitants of Scheria, ancient Corfu. There has been much development of hotels and apartments at Érmones in recent years. The Sunmarotel Érmones Beach Hotel has a funicular railway. Its track slices down the hillside between hotel bungalows and the beach; the ultimate hotel lift, undreamt of by Homer.

Érmones lies between two steep headlands, its shingle beach lapped by turquoise water. The Rópa River runs into the bay across the middle of the beach and this feature has strengthened the Homeric associations further. Here Nausicaa and her handmaidens came to wash clothes 'in the flowing stream of the lovely river', and, while playing a form of classical beach ball, discovered the exhausted Odysseus.

Today, beach ball is just one of Érmones' numerous activities, which include paragliding, and there are several tavernas above the beach. The beach shelves quickly into deep water and this should be kept in mind as far as young children and poor swimmers are concerned.

A rough path leads north from the road end above the beach, along the northern arm of the bay to the little Church of Zoodochos Pighi, the Source of Life. Here there are fine views to a lonely headland.

Inland from Érmones, on the flatlands of the Rópa Valley, is the Corfu Golf and Country Club, where a meandering stream adds zest to the course.

Gardíki

At the heart of the Gardíki area stands a ruin of a Byzantine fortress, the only historic site of note in the southern half of the island.

The Gardíki area lies between Mount Ágios Matthéos (► 20, 54) and Lake Korissíon (► 36), and boasts some remarkable historic remains. The most substantial is Gardíki Castle, a ruined Byzantine fortress, which probably dates from the early 13th century.

Near Gardíki Castle on the road from Parmonas and Cape Varka is the Grava Gardikiou rock shelter, dating from the Upper Palaeolithic period of 20,000BC, a time when a lower sea level meant that Corfu was part of what is now mainland Europe. During this period, early, primitive hunter-gatherers used such rock shelters while on hunting trips. Many stone tools and animal bones have been found at Grava Gardikiou and the site is currently accessible to the public. A prominent roadside notice board indicates the site, which is 400m uphill through olive groves. Orange arrows, on brown metal signs pinned to trees, point the way. The cave may seem mundane, but its antiquity creates a powerful sense of the past.

Lake Korissíon is reached by continuing from the fortress to where a side road leads to the north end of the lake. A short distance further on from the Lake Korissíon turn, a track leads down to the isolated Kanouli and Alonáki beaches.

INFORMATION

🔒 C2
✉ 25km south of Corfu Town. Reached from the main road about 1km beyond Messongí
🍴 Alonáki Beach taverna (€)
🚌 Green bus from Avramiou Street. Corfu Town–Ágios Matthéos. Get off at the Gardíki turn, then walk for 0.5km
🚗 Lake Korissíon (► 36)
🅿 Very limited roadside parking by castle

On the shore of Lake Korissíon, a large, shallow lake in the southwest of the island

[handwritten notes:] Walk to 2nd footpath to left of bay – as you look R.t. excellent caves

Kalámi

- B3
- Just off the main coast road, 30km north of Corfu Town
- The White House (€€)
- Green bus from Avramiou Street, Corfu Town–Kassiópi/Loútses
- Small ferry boats from nearby resorts
- None
- Kouloúra (➤ 54–55)
- Limited parking

Kalámi lies on Corfu's northeast coast, amid a landscape of quiet bays backed by the tree-clad slopes of Mount Pandokrator.

In the famous White House at Kalámi, the writer Lawrence Durrell lived for a time and there wrote his lyrical book *Prospero's Cell*. Today, Kalámi's idyllic peace and quiet, the 'charms of seclusion' described so vividly by Durrell, are no more. Seen from the north, however, its deep-blue bay caught within a green amphitheatre of olives and cypresses, the village still reflects the quintessential beauty of old Corfu. Unfortunately, the view from the south includes the modern terraced apartments that dominate the west side of the bay while continuing development has seen access roads to new villas gouged out of the green slopes.

The White House, 'set like a dice on a rock already venerable with the scars of wind and water', stands on the south side of the bay. It is distinctly English-looking, with its solid, square shape and its broad, hipped roof. Here Durrell and his wife, Nancy, lived what seems to have been a truly idyllic life in the Ionian sun. Their quickest way to Corfu Town was by boat and the Durrells travelled a great deal in their little sailing boat, the *Van Norden*. Their friends were a collection of serene eccentrics. Even the dynamic Henry Miller was persuaded to visit for a time and was captivated by Greece. Today, the White House functions as a taverna with apartments above.

Kalámi has a number of other tavernas, interspersed with villas, the whole softened by groves of orange and lemon trees, olives and cypresses. Although the resort is busy in summer, it is quiet in the evenings. Boats can be hired, and the beach is very safe for children.

The popular pebble beach at Kalámi

Kanóni

The resort lies at the southern tip of the Kanóni Peninsula overlooking the two little islands of Vlachérna and Pontikonísi (Mouse Island).

The view of Vlachérna, with its little convent and its solitary cypress tree, and of Pontikonísi, with its thicket of trees and its chapel, is probably the most photographed in the Ionian Islands, an enduring visual symbol of modern Corfu. The sounds accompanying this scenic delight are less soothing: Corfu's airport runway slices across the adjoining lagoon, Chalkiopoúlou, a few hundred metres away. (Youngsters will love plane-spotting.)

There is precedent for sound and fury, however. Kanóni is so named from being the site of a gun battery, first established by the French during the British blockade of Corfu from 1810 to 1815. Today, a Russian cannon, installed about 30 years ago to add colour, stands on the viewing terrace by the café and gift shop overlooking Vlachérna and Pontikonísi. Winding steps lead down from the terrace to the little harbour, from where Vlachérna is reached along a causeway. The Convent of the Virgin Mary here has a fine little Venetian belfry. Boats ferry visitors to Pontikonísi and run to and from Corfu Town. The little Byzantine Church of Pandokrator on Pontikonísi, said to date from the 11th or 12th century, has a characteristic octagonal dome and cross vaults, and a three-sided apse. Inside it is sparse and unadorned except for marble wall plaques recording past royal visits. The islet is one of the many candidates for being the ship turned to stone, by a jealous Poseidon, on its return from ferrying Odysseus to Ithaca.

INFORMATION

- ➕ B2
- ✉ At the southernmost tip of the Kanóni Peninsula, 5km south of Corfu Town
- 🍴 Kanoni (€–€€)
- 🚌 2 Kanóni. Blue bus from San Rocco Square
- ⛴ Caique ferries to and from Corfu Town
- ♿ None
- ❓ Limited parking by the viewing terrace. Follow parking signs on the approach road and branch right, signed Pontikonísi, to reach the unsurfaced harbourside car park

Trees dominate this tiny island just offshore from Corfu Town Airport, situated on the Kanóni peninsula

[handwritten annotations: take 2nd right, footpath at end; to bakeries, good toad/rd @ bay; left path in road; mon-beach. walk to left of Kassiópi harbour + fished in harb]

INFORMATION

- A3
- 37km north of Corfu Town on main coast road
- Large choice of snack bars and tavernas (€–€€)
- Green bus from Avramiou Street, Corfu Town–Kassiópi
- Ferry boats to and from Corfu Town. Excursions to other resorts
- Parking at harbour and at north end of resort by Kalamionas Beach

Lace bedspread, handmade in Kassiópi

The old port of Kassiópi lies within a picturesque setting of wooded promontories.

Today the village is a thriving resort – the main street and approach roads are crammed with cafés, bars, clubs and shops – but mixed in with all of this are important relics of its ancient past. There was a prehistoric settlement here and a Corinthian 'city' long before the Romans colonised the site. Beneath the village church lie the remains of a temple to Jupiter Cassius, from whom Kassiópi gets its name. Wealthy Romans came here for recreation, thus setting an ancient precedent for today's tourism. Among the visitors were Cato, Cicero and Tiberius. Even Nero passed through on his mad way to the Games at Corinth. The Romans fortified the headland above the harbour, and a castle was built in the 13th century by the Angevin rulers of Corfu. The Venetians, in their turn, wrecked this fortress and built one of their own, the broken walls of which still encircle the crown of the hill. Kassiópi's church is dedicated to the Blessed Virgin Kassiópitra, and possesses an icon of the Virgin that was credited at one time with having miraculous powers. This made the village a place of pilgrimage long before Spyrídon (▶9) became Corfu's patron saint.

Kassiópi is still a working fishing port and the harbour area has a lively atmosphere, especially in the mornings. The pebble beaches are small and hidden away behind headlands, whereas the larger Kalamionas Beach, and Imerolia Beach farther north, lie alongside the main road and have various watersports on offer.

Lefkímmi

Lefkímmi, or 'Ta Lefki' to locals, makes a refreshing contrast to resort Corfu and is characteristic of the south.

The far south of Corfu may have Kávos as a major resort, but the true character of the area is epitomised by the town of Lefkímmi – a straggle of communities, including Melikia, Potami, Anaplades and Ringlades, that have merged into one. It is the commercial centre of the south's farming and vine-growing area, and reflects the everyday life of the island beyond the beaches. Today, Lefkímmi is bypassed by a dual carriageway which hurtles south to Lefkímmi Port where it ends at the entrance to a vast quayside. From here ferries leave for Igoumenítsa on the mainland and for Paxoí (Paxos, ▶ 57).

Áno (Higher) Lefkímmi is the first part of the town entered from the main road when arriving from the north. By the roadside is the handsome Church of St Arsenios with domed bell-towers on either side of its arcaded façade. Arsenios (876–953) was the first Archbishop of Corfu; he was lionised when his efforts to dissuade Slav pirates from attacking Corfu led to the pirates imprisoning him. The outraged islanders promptly went to war against the Slavs, soundly thrashed them and freed the pacifist archbishop. Relics of St Arsenios are kept in the church.

From Áno Lefkímmi, a one-way system leads into the long main street of the town. The south end is dominated by the tall bell-tower of the Church of St Theodoros. Beyond is Potami, with the attractive 'Kampouli' Square and the River Himaros. The riverside roads lead south for 1.5km to the river mouth where there are small beaches and sand dunes.

INFORMATION

- 🔢 D2
- ✉️ 40km south of Corfu Town
- 🍴 Maria's Taverna, Potami (€)
- 🚌 Green bus from Avramiou Street, Corfu Town–Kávos
- ♿ Few
- ❓ Roadside parking. Lefkímmi Festival, 8 July

The twin domes of the Church of St Arsenios in Lefkímmi

Límni Korissión

INFORMATION

➕ C2

✉ On the west coast about 20km south of Corfu Town

🍴 Taverna (€) at north end of lake

🔁 Gardíki Castle (► 31)

❓ The north end of the lake is reached by following signposts for Gardíki from a junction about 1km south of Moraïtika. The south end is reached by turning west off the main road to Kávos, at Línia, and following signs for Paralía tou Íssou (Issos Beach)

Southwest Corfu is low-lying and Lake Korissión lies on the scimitar curve of the coast behind the remote Halikounas Beach.

Lake Korissión is a man-made lagoon of 607ha, created by the Venetians, who constructed a short, reinforced channel from the sea and flooded existing marshlands. It offers a peaceful respite from crowded beaches and the more popular resorts. Inland, the lake is bordered by low hills and, to the north, Mount Ágios Matthéos looms large. Even the ever-present olive relents here, to be replaced by silvery-green juniper and cedar trees that lie scattered along the lake shores and on the headlands, amid thickets of reeds. Flowering plants at Korissión include the spring catchfly, or loose-flowered orchid, with its purple blooms, just one of the dozen or so orchid species that flourish here. Summer sees the blue-green sea holly and various spurges; later in the season the beautiful white flowers of the sand lily, or sea daffodil, gleam in the dunes.

The lake and its margins provide an ideal winter habitat for birds. Over 120 species have been recorded here, including rare migrants such as the great white egret and the glossy ibis. Overwintering visitors include mallard, shelduck and teal, while waders such as greenshank, avocets and black-winged stilts are often in residence, along with the more common oystercatcher and curlew.

The neck of the channel at the entrance to the lake is blocked with fish traps to control the passage and catching of grey mullet – a rough track runs down the seaward edge of the lake from its northern end to a fish-watcher's hut beside the channel. One of the charms of Lake Korissión is its remoteness, and it has the bonus of a stretch of sandy beach north and south of the channel.

Moraïtika

The name Moraïtika sounds convincingly Hawaiian and the resort does its best to live up to the image. The only thing missing is the surf.

Continuing the Hawaiian theme, Moraïtika's beach has more exotic palms and thatched umbrellas to the square metre than you can throw a Malibu board at.

Like Benítses, Moraïtika is made up of old and new. Áno (Upper) Moraïtika, a delightful complex of old houses, modern villas, and a couple of tavernas, all happily swamped in bougainvillaea, is tucked away on the high ground above the north end of the resort.

The resort proper runs to the south of here, the dusty main road lined with restaurants, tavernas, bars, clubs, cafés and shops. Between road and sea is a broad swathe of land, dotted with villas and hotels, that runs down to Moraïtika's long stretch of sun-trapping sand and shingle beach. The southern end of the beach is dominated by the very large Messongí Beach Hotel, which has its own gymnasium, tennis court, swimming pools, restaurants, beach taverna, café and shopping centre. There are watersports in plenty at Moraïtika, including gentler alternatives for children. The beach even has freshwater shower points and a changing stall at its midpoint.

Working barge in the sheltered harbour at Moraïtika

INFORMATION

- 🔆 C2
- ✉ 20km south of Corfu Town, on main coast road
- 🍴 Cafés and tavernas on beach and in main street (€–€€)
- 🚌 Green bus from Avramiou Street, Corfu Town–Kávos and Corfu Town–Messongí
- 🚤 Excursion boats from beach
- 🔁 Benítses (➤ 28) and Messongí (➤ 53)
- 🅿 Parking in main street

Mouseío Archaiologikó

INFORMATION

- B2
- 1 Vraila Armeni Street
- (26610) 30680
- Tue–Sun 8.30–3
- Cafés and tavernas in nearby San Rocco Square (€) and on the Liston (€€€)
- Excellent
- Moderate. Free on Sun

Detail of the Gorgon Pediment (585 BC), discovered near the temple of Artemis at Kanóni

Corfu Town's Archaeological Museum houses some outstanding relics from the island's ancient past.

The museum contains one of the finest prehistoric relics in all of Greece, the famous Gorgon pediment recovered from the ruins of the 6th-century BC Temple of Artemis on the Kanóni Peninsula. Though it is not intact, the pediment, 17m long and 3m high, has been restored skilfully. Such monumental antiquity may seem incidental to devoted beach lovers, but the impact of the snake-haired, eye-popping Medusa sheltering her blood offspring, Chrysaor and Pegasus, attended by Zeus and slaughtered Titans and flanked by leopards, is enough to draw breath from the most jaded onlooker. The glaring eyes seem to follow you about the room.

The Gorgon frieze is matched, in the South Hall, by the splendid Lion of Menekrates, a limestone sculpture of the late 7th century BC. Discovered in 1843, it is considered to be one of the finest examples of early Corinthian art, a fluid and life-like creation. Gaze long enough and you begin to suspect that the lion may leap.

Other delights include some excellent tomb monuments, classical pottery and Bronze Age artefacts, and an impressive collection of coins dating from the 6th to 3rd centuries BC. In the North Hall there are some splendid terracotta fittings and artefacts from the ruins of a 7th-century temple found in the grounds of Mon Repos villa.

The finest exhibit here is the left side of a limestone pediment featuring the god Dionysus and a naked youth, well supplied with wine and reclining on a couch. Both are avidly watching a scene on the lost half of the pediment, a tantalising omission for the rest of us.

Mouseío Vizantinó

This remarkable and outstanding collection of Byzantine art dates from the 16th century.

The Church of Panagia Antivouniotissa (Church of the Blessed Virgin – the name Antivouniotissa comes from the hill on which the church stands), houses the collection. There are about 90 icons on display, most from the 13th to the 17th centuries and depicting individual saints and biblical scenes. There is also outstanding work by the celebrated Cretan painters Emanuel Tzanes and Michael Damaskinos, among others.

The plain outside walls of the church mask a beautiful interior of enclosed arcades surrounding a central nave with a wonderful coffered and decorated ceiling, painted walls and gilded woodwork. From the centre of the nave, the view through the glass entrance door to Vídos Island in the distance makes an exquisite picture.

INFORMATION

🚑 B2
✉ Arseniou (Mourayia)
☎ (26610) 38313
🕐 Tue–Sun 8.30–3
🍴 Cafés, restaurants (€–€€) in Old Port Square, Faliraki (€€)
🅿 Moderate
❓ Exhibits generally labelled in English as well as Greek

On the steps of Corfu's Byzantine Museum

Myrtiótissa (Mirtiotissa)

INFORMATION

+ B1
* 12km west of Corfu Town. Reached down a 1km rough track (not suitable for cars), signposted from the Glyfáda road, or by 2.5km path from the village of Vátos
* Snack bar on beach (€) summer only and Myrtiótissa restaurant (€) uphill from the beach
* Green bus from Avramiou Street, Corfu Town–Vátos
* Excursion boats arrive from other resorts
* Parking at beach is very limited

Monastery
* 8–1, 5–8

This lovely spot has avoided development because of the difficult access and looming cliffs behind the beach.

Beautiful Myrtiótissa, with its backdrop of tree-covered cliffs, was once a genuine 'Desert Island' beach, praised by Lawrence Durrell for its 'lion-gold' sand. It is very popular with an entertaining mix of devotees. The south end is favoured by nudists. The only blot here is the line of telegraph poles and wires that lead to the little Monastery of the Blessed Virgin Myrtiótissa. This lies at the end of a track that runs past the solitary Bella Vista Taverna. It was founded in response to the discovery, in a myrtle bush, of an abandoned icon of the Virgin. The monastery building has very fine arched doorways and carved keystones, which contrast charmingly with the used food cans that serve as flowerpots in the forecourt.

The beach at Myrtiótissa shelves slightly and there are offshore reefs and rocks of very rough conglomerate. A makeshift snack bar operates on the beach in summer. Be aware of currents.

The wide stretch of sands of Myrtiótissa Beach

Paláti tou Agíou Michaíl tou Georgíou

Dominating the Plateía the palace is the most striking relic of the 50-year British presence on Corfu.

INFORMATION

- B2
- Spianáda (Esplanade)
- (26610) 38124
- Tue–Sun 8.30–3
- Art Gallery Café (€)
- Moderate
- Esplanade (▶ 48)

The palace was built at the northern end of the Esplanade, between 1819 and 1824 during the service of Sir Thomas Maitland, the first High Commissioner, and was used as the official seat of the Protectorate. The palace is triumphantly neo-classical in style, the first building of its kind to be built in modern Greece, with a passing nod to the Parthenon in its Doric portico. In the landscaped garden in front of the palace stands a statue of Sir Frederick Adam, second High Commissioner.

The palace was the venue for the EC Summit of 1994. The interior is outstanding: the finest feature is the rotunda on the first floor, its domed ceiling painted in blue and gold, its walls punctuated with mahogany doors, niches and mirrored panels.

Several of the state rooms house the Museum of Asiatic Art, a remarkable collection of Sino-Japanese art and artefacts, including mosaics from the early Christian Basilica of Palaiopolis. Chinese and Japanese exhibits make up the largest part of the collection but there are also objects from India, Tibet, Nepal, Korea and Thailand. Items include prehistoric bronzes, porcelain ware, woodcarvings, Noh theatre masks, wood and brass statuettes, Samurai armour and weapons, screens, fans and much more. The main bulk of the collection was given to the Greek government in 1926 by the Corfiot-born diplomat Gregorios Manos (1850–1929). The palace also houses the Municipal Art Gallery (▶ 56) and the Modern Art Museum, with a small collection of Greek contemporary art.

Sir Thomas Maitland, first High Commissioner of the Ionian Islands

41

Palaiokastrítsa (Paleokastritsa)

INFORMATION

✚ B1

✉ On the west coast of Corfu, 25km from Corfu Town

🍴 Numerous tavernas and cafés in resort

🚌 Green bus from Avramiou Street, Corfu Town–Paleokastritsa

🚤 Boat trips to view coastal features, caves and grottoes

♿ None

↔ Angelókastro (➤ 27)

Monastery

🕐 8–1, 3–8

🍴 Café (€€) outside monastery

💷 A small donation appreciated

❓ Dress appropriately when visiting the monastery

The stunning sheltered harbour of Paleokastritsa

The wooded headlands and crescent-shaped bays of Corfu's most celebrated scenic extravaganza have attracted visitors since the early 19th century.

At Paleokastritsa, towering mountains give way reluctantly to the sea, their tree-clad slopes mottled with great cliffs. Here, the landscape has overwhelmed the human element, instead of the other way round. Roads end at Paleokastritsa, giving a real sense of arrival.

Long before the British holidaymaker first picnicked at 'Paleo', the western headland was home to a monastery dedicated to the Virgin Mary. The original foundation was 13th-century, but the present complex is mainly 18th-century. A small church lies at the bone-white heart of the monastery, its walls laden with icons in chunky rococo frames; a fine painting of the Last Judgement hangs above the south doorway. Lemon trees and bougainvillaea soften the hard brilliance outside, and from the garden terrace there is a breathtaking view across the Bay of Liapádes to Cape Ágios Iliodoros and on to distant Cape Plaka. Within the monastery complex is a preserved oil mill and a small museum displaying icons, and a collection of shells and bones from the sea.

The less spiritual delights of Paleokastritsa include the rather cramped, sun-trap beaches of Ágios Spyrídon, which lie to either side of the main car park. The harbour and beaches at Alipo Bay lie beyond the easterly headland of St Nicholas. There are sun-loungers and watersports equipment, and boats can be hired from the harbour. Organised boat trips visit nearby cliff grottoes and caves, and the crystal-clear seas round 'Paleo' are especially good for scuba diving.

Pantokrátoras (Pandokratoras)

The mountain's vast bulk, and its rolling hinterland of *maquis* dense with kermes oak, myrtle and wild flowers, creates a persuasive sense of wilderness and open space.

Pandokrator, at 906m a spectacular viewpoint, was known in prehistory as Istone and by the Venetians as Monte San Salvatore. In the 14th century a church dedicated to Christ Pandocrator, 'The Almighty' or 'The All Embracing One', was built on the summit of the mountain and the name was eventually applied to the entire massif. The present buildings are 19th-century replacements of earlier structures. Today, the monastery shares the crowded summit, rather uneasily, with a huge radio mast and various other beacons and aerials. There is a pilgrimage to the monastery on 6 August each year to celebrate the Feast of the Transfiguration.

From the north the approach is by road, through Néa (New) Períthia (▶ 45) and then by a track to join the summit road. The best approach, however, is from the south through Spartýas and the village of Strinýas. Just beyond Strinýas, bear right at a junction and on to a good road which leads to the summit. The last kilometre, surfaced with ribbed concrete, is extremely tortuous and steep. Parking space at the summit is limited. It may be more practical, and in some ways more fitting, to walk the last section from roadside parking below the summit. Experienced hillwalkers, with proper clothing, footwear and equipment, will find off-road exploration of the mountain rewarding.

INFORMATION

✚ A3
✉ Dominates the northeast corner of the island, 37km north of Corfu Town
🍴 Café outside monastery gate
💷 Monastery free, small donation welcome
❓ Roadside parking about 1km from the summit near the junction with the track from Néa (New) Períthia, signposted Pyrgí, Róda and Kassiópi

The dimly lit interior of a church near the 906m summit of Mount Pantokrator

Pélekas

INFORMATION

➕ B2

✉ 13km from Corfu Town
on west coast

🍽 Jimmy's (€€)

🚌 Blue bus No 11 from San
Rocco Square, Corfu
Town–Pélekas

↔ Glyfáda (➤ 52–53)

❓ Limited parking in village.
Parking at viewpoint

This hilltop village has evolved into an inland tourist resort because of its proximity to popular beaches.

Nearby Glyfáda on the coast and small beaches, such as Kontoyialos and Gialiskari, can be reached down steep lanes and tracks. Above the village, a famous viewpoint, known variously as the Kaiser's Lookout, Tower or Throne, has added to the busy trail of summer visitors. It was to this hilltop that Kaiser Wilhelm II motored frequently from the Achilleion Palace (➤ 24) to admire the spectacular sunsets off the west coast. The viewpoint is reached by following a steep road signposted from the centre of Pélekas. Just before the summit, the road passes between the tiny whitewashed Church of the Virgin of the Annunciation and its bell-tower. There is parking at the road end, from where a paved path leads under a little archway and on through trees to the circular viewpoint with its railing and seats. The

Luxuriant foliage on a balcony in a hill village near Pélekas

views are spectacular; east to Corfu Town and Vídos Island; northwest along the green trough of the Rópa Valley; south to Mount Ágios Matthéos; and west across a green wooded landscape to the western sea. Bring your own binoculars; the mounted pair at the lookout may not work.

Pélekas itself retains the charm of a typical Corfiot hill village, although development has begun to erode its traditional character. There are several tavernas and cafés, plus numerous shops and tourist agencies. In the central square, with its war memorial and well-kept church, an old sea mine, now painted blue and white, serves as an eccentric plant pot.

Perítheia (Perithia)

This is the most impressive of Corfu's abandoned villages and farmsteads and is gradually being revived.

INFORMATION

- A3
- 50km from Corfu Town on northern slopes of Mount Pandokrator. Reached from coast road at Néa Períthia
- Foros (€€)
- Limited parking by road end

In the hidden hollows of Mount Pandokrator's upper slopes lie the ruins of old farmsteads and villages. They were established originally by Corfu's Byzantine peoples fleeing repeated pirate raids on their coastal settlements. Abandoned villages can also be found at Old Siniés and at Rou on the east side of the mountain. Today, the shells of houses are being refurbished, and summer tavernas cater for visitors.

Perithia can be reached by the mountain road from Néa (New) Perithia, which lies on the coast road between Kassiópi and Acharávi. About 5km along this mountain road from Néa Períthia, a rough track leads off left from a steep right-hand bend on the surfaced road. (This track eventually joins the road from Strinýlas to the summit of Mount Pandokrator.) For Old Perithia, keep on the surfaced road to an old church at the entrance to the village, where there is limited parking.

The framework of Perithia survives within its setting of terraced fields and scattered stands of cherry, almond, oak and walnut trees. Empty houses, complete with outside staircases and the stone brackets of missing balconies, retain their shutters and tiled roofs. But doors and windows gape, and floorboards sag alarmingly; it is dangerous to enter. At the heart of the village a cobbled lane descends to the central square, where there are two summer tavernas.

The bell-tower of one of the many chapels that are scattered about the tiny village of Perithia

follow signs for Canal d'Amour, O.K. Beach. (small)

Sidári

INFORMATION

🚩 A2
✉ 36km from Corfu Town on north coast
🍴 Cafés and tavernas (€–€€)
🚌 Green bus from Avramiou Street, Corfu Town–Róda–Sidári
🚢 Excursions by boat to Kassiópi, Paleokastritsa and the Diapondía Islands, sea conditions permitting
♿ Flat access to Megali Beach. Flat access to edge of official Canal d'Amour Beach
🔄 Perouládes (➤ 55), Róda (➤ 53)
❓ Parking behind main street. Main street is one way

Flower-fringed church of St Nicholas in Sidári

First settled in neolithic times, Sidári is now Corfu's main west-coast resort with excellent beaches.

The beaches at Sidári include the large Megali Beach at the southern entrance to the resort and the smaller Canal d'Amour beaches below the sculpted sandstone cliffs of Sidári's north-facing coast. There is shallow water and safe bathing here, with every beachside facility to hand; watersports in plenty, a big water slide, go-karts, and numerous restaurants, tavernas, bars and clubs.

Halfway along the long main street is a little village square, a brave fragment of old Sidári amid the glare of tourism. Here, beneath plane trees that have their trunks painted white to guard against disease, are little seats, a sea-horse fountain, and a bandstand wreathed in bougainvillaea and geraniums. On the north side of the square is the cream and white Church of St Nicholas, its porch hung with lamps and with an icon painted on its domed interior.

At the northern end of the main street a bridge crosses the Loxida River and the road beyond runs west past villas and hotels. Lanes between the buildings on the north side lead to beaches which all claim to be the location of the famous Canal d'Amour. The image of this 'Channel of Love' has worn as thin as the original sea arch that gave rise to the name and which has long since collapsed. Tradition claimed that if you swam through the original arch, various romantic events would result. Today, the official Canal d'Amour is said to be an eroded inlet at the most easterly beach on the north-facing coast. On the other hand, some say it is the channel between a pair of sea stacks further west, where the little beaches of Vithismeno, Apotripiti and Atri vie for attention.

Sinarádes

This is a traditional Corfiot village, part Venetian, part Byzantine, and with an authentic flavour of island life.

In the main street there is a medieval bell-tower of unpainted stone, its twin bells still in place. The village square is attractive, with huge palm trees, a small bandstand and a fountain featuring statues of rearing horses. Sinarádes has its own Philharmonic Orchestra and the square is the focus of some excellent local festivals.

A short distance along the main street south from the square is the Church of St Nicholas. Opposite, a signpost points the way up a paved alley to the delightful Folklore Museum of Central Corfu, a two-storeyed building reached by a narrow stairway. Part of the building is a reconstruction of a 19th-century village house with furnishings and utensils. Exhibits include farming tools, musical instruments and traditional costumes.

INFORMATION

- ✚ C2
- ✉ 15km from Corfu Town on the west coast
- 🍴 Cafés and tavernas (€–€€)
- 🚌 Green bus from Avramiou Street, Corfu Town–Sinarádes–Ágios Górdis
- ♿ None
- ⬕ Ágios Górdis (➤ 51)

Folklore Museum of Central Corfu
- ☎ (26610) 54962
- 🕐 All year Tue–Sun 9.30–2.30. Opening hours are flexible
- ♿ None
- 🎟 Cheap

Plants decorate the steps to the Sinarádes' Folklore Museum

The Spianáda (Esplanade) and the Liston

INFORMATION

* B2
* Numerous café/restaurants (€€–€€€) on the Liston
* Good access
* Free
* Paláti tou Agíou Michaíl tou Georgíou (➤ 41)

Corfu Town's Esplanade is one of the most charming urban open spaces in the Mediterranean.

The Spianáda is a public arena for relaxed promenading, for reading newspapers, for quiet gossip over Greek or iced coffee, orange juice or ouzo, for carnival and festival, and for the joy of uninterrupted summer sunshine from morning till night.

The Esplanade owes its open nature to the Venetians, who cleared the medieval town that lay in front of the fortress. They ensured that the line of their buildings along the western edge of this open ground incorporated numerous straight alleyways to allow direct lines of fire from the Old Fortress to defend against potential attack from the landward side.

These buildings survive along Kapodistriou Street, but on the Plateía, the northern section of the Esplanade, the terrace of arcaded buildings known as the Liston was built by the French in the style of the Parisian rue de Rivoli. Today, with its generally expensive, but stylish, cafés and restaurants, the Liston is a focus for Corfu Town at play, a venue for a colourful mix of gregarious locals, visitors and fashion-conscious youngsters on parade. At the far end of the Esplanade is the wide green space used for cricket matches. The game is a legacy of the British who also left a taste for *tsin tsin birra* – ginger beer.

The southern half of the Esplanade is landscaped with flowerbeds and a fountain, and an elegant bandstand where the town's brass bands perform on summer Sunday afternoons. At its far end is the Perist lio Maitland (Maitland Rotunda), a rather battered classical memorial built in honour of Sir Thomas Maitland, the first High Commissioner during the British Protectorate.

Café in the arcaded Liston, on the western edge of the Esplanade (Spianáda) in the heart of Corfu town

CORFU'S
best

Corfu's Best

Beach Resorts

WATER SAFETY

Some beaches in Corfu have a system of safety signals that indicate whether or not prevailing conditions are safe for watersports or swimming. Signals may vary. If any signal, usually a coloured flag, is displayed, its significance should be checked and its instruction heeded.

ACHARÁVI (AHARAVI)

This popular family resort on Corfu's north coast lies a short distance inland from the beach and to either side of the wide main road. The wooded heights of Mount Pandokrator rise impressively behind and a different world of dense olive groves and quiet villages, such as Epískepsi and Láfki, can be reached from the resort. Acharavi has a range of shops and eating places. Villas and hotels fill the space between village and seafront. The sand and shingle beach shelves gently and bathing is safe. Watersports and beachside tavernas.

✉ 38km north of Corfu Town, on north coast main road 🍴 Beachside tavernas and cafés (€–€€) 🚌 Green bus from Avramiou Street, Corfu Town–Acharávi ♿ Beach accessible from seafront road

AFIÓNAS

The road ends at Afiónas. To the south of the village lies a narrow promontory that ends at Ákrotírio (Cape) Aríllas, while to the west lies Kravía (Gravia) Island, the 'Ship Island', with its little flotilla of offshore rocks trailing behind it. Just in front of the church at Afiónas, a surfaced lane leads off towards the cape. In 50m, at a junction, the lane bears right (signed Dionysos Taverna). Keep left along a rough track that leads out onto the promontory and down to a narrow neck of land at Porto Timoni. Small beaches lie to either side. On the headland are the faint remains of defensive walls dating from about 500 BC.

✉ On headland on northwest coast 🍴 Three Brothers Taverna (€€) just before entrance to village 🚌 Green bus from Avramiou Street, Corfu Town– Magouládes–Afiónas. Not Sun

Pedaloes and a warning flag on the long stretch of beach at Ágios Geórgios

ÁGIOS GEÓRGIOS (NORTHWEST)

Ágios Geórgios is an attractive coast resort and although its individuality has been blurred by beachfront development, bold, natural surroundings still dominate the scene. The sandy beach sweeps for over 2km along the curve of a south-facing bay between Ákrotírio (Cape) Aríllas and Ákrotírio (Cape) Falakron. Bathing is safe here, although the area can be windy at times, making Ágios Geórgios a good windsurfing centre. There are windsurfing schools on the beach as well as jet-ski and waterski facilities.

✉ On shores of bay on northwest coast 🍴 Tavernas and restaurants (€–€€) throughout the resort 🚌 Green bus from Avramiou Street, Corfu Town–Ágios Geórgios

ÁGIOS GEÓRGIOS (SOUTHWEST)

Like its northern namesake, this Ágios Geórgios has been tacked on to a long stretch of sandy beach, part of the almost continuous 12km strand that fringes the southwest shoreline of Corfu. Linear development has left the resort without much heart, but location is what matters. Numerous watersports are available and several good tavernas overlook the sand. The beach is narrow, but you can find uncrowded space if you walk some distance along the open coast in either direction. Inland is the village of Argyrádes (Argirades), worth visiting for its friendly, down-to-earth atmosphere, its Venetian architecture and its shops and cafés.

✉ On the southwest coast 🍴 Several good restaurants and tavernas (€–€€) or Kafesas (€€€) for seafood at the south end of the resort 🚌 Green bus from Avramiou Street, Corfu Town–Argirades–Ágios Geórgios

ÁGIOS GÓRDIS

An attractive west-coast resort at the foot of spectacular pine-covered coastal hills where the beach is framed by big headlands to north and south. At the beach's northern end are Plitiri Point and the rocky heights of Aerostato, known at one time as 'The Lookout' because of its use as a watch-point for pirates and potential invaders. Just offshore from Ágios Górdis's southern headland is a remarkable tusk-like pinnacle called the Ortholith. Onshore is a similar pinnacle, beyond which rises the great bulk of Mount Garoúna. The beach is wide and sandy with patches of shingle, and numerous watersports are available, including a beachside diving centre. A steep hike to the south from Ágios Górdis takes you to the rocky cove of Fieroula and on to the hamlet of Pentátion.

✉ 17km southwest of Corfu Town 🍴 Cafés and tavernas (€–€€) throughout the resort 🚌 Green bus from Avramiou Street, Corfu Town–Ágios Górdis

ÁGIOS STÉFANOS (NORTHWEST)

Corfu's other Ágios Stéfanos is a popular family resort set on the shores of a wide bay with a large, flat expanse of beach and high white cliffs at the northern end of the bay. The resort, custom-built with villas, hotels, tavernas, bars and shops lining the beachfront, is named after the Chapel of San Stefano, which stands on a small promontory to the south of the beach. Beyond the chapel lies a large working harbour full of fishing caiques and excursion boats. There is safe bathing at the beach, which is crossed at its mid-point by a rather marshy river, and all types of beach equipment are on offer. Watersports include waterskiing and paragliding, and trips can be arranged to the neaby Diapondía Islands (➤ 42) and south to Paleokastritsa (➤ 57).

✉ 45km from Corfu Town on northwest coast 🍴 Manthos (€€) 🚌 Green bus from Avramiou Street, Corfu Town–Sidári–Ágios Stéfanos ♿ Flat access to beach

SAFE BEACHES

Most of Corfu's beaches have safe bathing, with shallow water extending for some distance over sand and shingle and with an absence of currents. Where steep shelving occurs on beaches, or where there may be potentially dangerous currents, this is mentioned in the text. Tidal movements in the Mediterranean generally are minimal, although there may be some visible change in the waterline, especially on the west-coast beaches. At some beaches, more sand builds up, or is exposed, in summer.

One of two villages on Corfu called Ágios Stefanos; this one is on the island's east coast

51

ÁKROTÍRIO KOMMÉNO (CAPE KOMMÉNO)

The wooded promontory of Cape Komméno encloses a small south-facing bay at the northern end of the larger Gouviá Bay. Hotels and villas are at the top end of the price range, and there is a whiff of exclusiveness in the air. Several manufactured beaches lie along the wooded shores, but they are small and monopolised by hotel guests. In 1537 and 1716, Turkish armies landed in the Cape Komméno and Gouviá area in ultimately unsuccessful bids to capture Venetian Corfu.

✉ 11km north of Corfu Town. Reached from coast road north of Gouviá just after branching right from the road to Paleokastritsa 🍴 There are a number of good-quality restaurants (€€–€€€) 🅿 Limited parking

BARMPÁTI (BARBATI)

At Barbati the steep slopes of Mount Pandokrator crowd the shoreline. Behind the beach and the main road the rocky flanks of the mountain rise from dense olive groves, creating an impressive backdrop. Barbati has a long, silvery-white, shingle beach – a striking contrast to the azure sea. The beach is ideal for youngsters because it offers safe and sheltered bathing, and lies far enough below the road to escape traffic noise. There are watersports in plenty, including waterskiing, windsurfing and parascending, plus pedaloes and dinghies. The village has supermarkets, gift shops and tavernas. Nightlife is limited to quiet drinks and meals; the only thing missing on this eastern shore is a view of the sunset. But there's always the sunrise…

✉ 20km north of Corfu Town. Beach is reached down slip road at south entrance to resort 🍴 Lord Byron (€€) 🚌 Green bus from Avramiou Street, Corfu Town—Kassiópi

DASIÁ (DASSIÁ)

Dassiá's shingle beach is spared the roadside clamour of other resorts, but its popularity and proximity to Corfu Town makes the seafront a busy place. A zone of hotels and apartments lies between the beach and the main road which has the bulk of gift shops, tavernas and services, as well as the lavish frontages of two big hotels, the Corfu Chandris and the Dasiá Chandris. There is a popular campsite inland from the main road. The beach's shallow waters, reached down narrow lanes, make it safe for young children. Wooden jetties run seaward to cater for the excursion boats that arrive loaded with day visitors and leave for trips. All types of watersports, including waterskiing and paragliding, add to the bustle, and there are various beachfront café-bars and tavernas.

✉ 13km north of Corfu Town on main road 🍴 Choice of cafés, snack bars on beach (€–€€) 🚌 Blue bus No 7 from San Rocco Square, Corfu Town—Dassiá 🅿 Roadside parking

GLYFÁDA (GLIFADA)

Glifada, one of the finest beaches on the west coast of Corfu, with a long stretch of golden sand, is reached down a winding road. There has been much

The tall trees on Dassiá beach reach almost to the water's edge

development here and major hotels tend to dominate the backdrop of tree-covered coastal hills. Watersports are available, and include sailing and windsurfing. The beach shelves steeply in places, but otherwise Glifada is the kind of sandy paradise adored by youngsters. There are tavernas lining the beachfront and these popular venues go non-stop until late at night. You'll find peace along tracks and paths to the north and south of the resort.

✉ 16km from Corfu Town 🍴 Beachside tavernas (€–€€) 🚌 Green bus from Avramiou Street, Corfu Town–Vátos–Glyfáda 🚌 Pélekas (► 44) 🅿 Car park behind beach

KONTÓKALI (KONDOKALI)

Kondokali, the first resort to the north of Corfu Town, is fast becoming the service centre for the expanding marina that takes up the adjoining shoreline. The resort has excellent restaurants, tavernas and bars. The narrow pebble beaches become crowded in summer. Extended and modernised, the marina has capacity for over 800 boats and is now equipped with most services and facilities, including car rental. It is the island's main base for yacht chartering.

✉ 7km north of Corfu Town 🍴 Restaurants and snack bars (€–€€) 🚌 Blue bus No 7, from San Rocco Square, Corfu Town–Kondokali–ouviá–Dassiá 🅿 Few 🅿 Limited roadside parking

MESONGÍ (MESSONGÍ)

Separated from Moraïtika by the Messongí River, Messongí is the first resort south of Corfu Town to escape from the main road. The coast sweeps away in a gentle curve to the south where tree-covered hills fill the horizon. Although the sand and shingle beach is very narrow, it has safe bathing and is an ideal spot for families. A narrow road, packed with shops and tavernas, leads from the north end of the beach to the river bank.

✉ 22km south of Corfu Town 🍴 Cafés and tavernas (€–€€) 🚌 Green bus from Avramiou Street, Corfu Town–Kávos or Corfu Town–Messongí 🚤 Excursion boats to other resorts 🅿 Roadside parking

RÓDA

North-coast Róda is a pleasant resort with safe bathing and a handful of tavernas and clubs. The main road passes some distance inland from the beach, and between the two, intensive hotel and villa development has taken place. A little harbour within a rough breakwater marks the original fishing village, and fishing caiques still work from here. Róda's beach, narrow and sandy, with rocky patches, is backed by tavernas, cafés, gift shops and clubs. Part way up the main street is the Church of Ágios Geórgios, in an attractive square dotted with lemon trees and plane trees.

✉ On north coast, 37km north of Corfu Town 🍴 Cafés and tavernas (€–€€) 🚌 Green bus from Avramiou Street, Corfu Town–Róda 🅿 Seafront road alongside beach 🅿 Limited parking at seafront

KAVOS

Kávos is Corfu's premier resort for loud and lively holidaymaking, although no one is too lively at midday thanks to late-night sessions in the numerous bars. This is emphatically a young persons' place, but its long (over 2km) sandy beach, safe bathing and varied watersports make it popular with families, too. Old Kávos survives in the form of a handful of real fishing boats moored offshore. Kávos has dozens of bars and clubs, and the first thing anyone who is looking for local colour will notice is the total absence of the Greek language on signs and billboards. But in anyone's language, the beach is still a great place to enjoy all that Mediterranean sun. The sand finally relents in the south, where low cliffs begin. Kávos is 45km south of Corfu Town. Beyond are the lonelier reaches of Ákrotíro (Cape) Asprókavos, if you feel in need of some solitude.

MISCELLANEOUS ATTRACTIONS

There are numerous boat excursions from the larger resorts. Regular ferries ply between the Old Port and Vídos Island. *The Calypso Star*, a glass-bottomed boat, runs trips round the island from the Old Port. In Corfu Town, on the Esplanade, trips can be made in horse-drawn carriages.

Towns and Villages

ÁGIOS MATTAÍOS (ÁGIOS MATTHEOS)

Ágios Mattheos, one of the largest and most traditional of Corfu's mountain villages, is built on a series of terraces on the tree-covered slopes of the 463m Mount Ágios Mattheos, known locally as Grava. Near the top of the mountain is the 4th-century Monastery of Pandokrator, now abandoned but cared for by villagers. On 6 August each year a religious festival is held here through the night. A paved lane winds through the heart of the village to a wide square with a fountain and a well-kept church. The view east across the island from here is exhilarating.

✉ 22km southwest of Corfu Town 🍴 Snack bars (€) in main street
🚌 Green bus from Avramiou Street, Corfu Town–Ágios Mattheos
❓ Small car park on the northern edge of the village

ÁNO KORAKIÁNA

Áno, or upper, Korakiána is a handsome hill village with a strong Venetian element to its buildings and its churches; it even has its own Philharmonic Society. The village lies along the tree-covered foothills of the western massif of Mount Pandokrator. The Church of St Athanasios has an 18th-century fresco of St Spyrídon and St Athanasios banishing a dragon, the symbol of a 4th-century plague. At the village's midpoint is the entertaining façade of a house displaying the highly diverting sculptures of local 'popular' artist Arestides Zach Metallinos.

✉ 18km northwest of Corfu Town 🍴 Cafés in village (€) 🚌 Green bus from Avramiou Street, Corfu Town–Korakiána

DOUKÁDES

This archetypal Corfiot mountain village is spectacularly sited beneath limestone crags, with a steep hinterland of lovely olive groves. Viewed from the Troumbetas Pass road, the great cliff above the clustered village seems to hang in mid-air. Doukádes has a pretty central square with adjacent tavernas and shops and there are seats alongside the Church of the Blessed Virgin Mesochoritissa, notable for its splendid doorcases and doors. Numerous Venetian buildings of great style grace the village.

✉ 18km northwest of Corfu. From the Paleokastritsa road, go through village to a little car park reached down a slip road to the left
🍴 Elizabeth's Taverna (€) 🚌 Green bus from Avramiou Street, Corfu Town–Paleokastritsa, then short steep walk

A Greek lady outside the door of her immaculately kept house in the town of Doukádes

KOULOÚRA

Kouloúra is a close neighbour to Kalámi, but has a rare sense of exclusiveness, partly because there is no beach to speak of. Excursion boats visit Kouloúra, whose name derives from the Greek for 'ring shape', like that of the tiny bay set against a backdrop of poker-straight cypresses and feathery pines. Its charm is enhanced by the curve of a harbour breakwater that shelters fishing boats, and by its focal point, the handsome house that stands on the site of an ancient fortress and retains the bell-tower of a medieval chapel. On calm days, the Corfu Channel between here and Albania can seem like an inland lake.

✉ 31km north of Corfu Town 🍴 Tavernas at Kálami (€€)
🛳 Excursion boats visit

MAKRÁDES
The village of Makrádes lies on the road north from Paleokastritsa and works very hard at being the retail hub of the known world. Roadside stalls and their insistent traders, selling everything from embroidered table linen to knitwear, ceramics and carpets, lie in wait for summer coach parties while tavernas and cafés help you to get rid of the small change. It's a place to try out your haggling ability.

✉ 35km northwest of Corfu Town 🍴 Cafés and tavernas (€€)
🚌 Green bus from Avramiou Street, Corfu Town–Makrádes

PERIVÓLI
This is a down-to-earth farming village, with narrow lanes and alleyways. The church here is called Agii Saranda, the Forty Saints. Perivóli has a number of traditional *kafenions* and tavernas where only aficionados of Greek living will feel at ease. The village is the gateway to several accessible points on the great sweep of beach that runs down the southwest coast including Paralía Gardénos (Vitaládes Beach) reached through the village of Vitaládes and Paralía Agías Varváras (Santa Barbara Beach).

✉ 35km south of Corfu Town, on main road south to Lefkimmi and Kávos 🍴 Tavernas at Vitaládes Beach and at Santa Barbara Beach (€)
🚌 Green bus from Avramiou Street, Corfu Town–Kávos

PEROULÁDES
Corfu's northwestern limits are marked by the dramatic white cliffs of Ákrotírio Drástis, near the village of Perouládes, which rise sheer from the sea to heights of over 50m in places. Long, narrow fins of rock jut out from the shore and gentler promontories, patched with scrub, mark the far points of land. From the village square, a narrow road runs west between huddled buildings. A few metres along the road a lane goes steeply uphill to the right, leading past the village school and church and on to Ákrotírio Drástis. Although surfaced at first, the lane soon becomes very rough; driving is not advised. The track leads in about 1.5km to a dramatic viewpoint overlooking the Diapondía Islands. The narrow road at Perouládes leads through the village to a right turning, signposted Longas Beach. This leads shortly to the Panorama Taverna, from where concrete steps descend to a narrow beach below towering cliffs.

✉ 45km from Corfu Town 🍴 Panorama (€€) 🚌 Green bus from Avramiou Street, Corfu Town– Sidári–Perouládes–Ágios Stéfanos

A local woman, dressed in the traditional black, in the village of Perivóli

Museums & Galleries

DIMOTIKÍ PINAKOTHÍKI (MUNICIPAL ART GALLERY)

This delightful gallery was opened in 1995 in the east
wing of the Palace of St Michael and St George. The
exhibition rooms are a pleasure in themselves, and the
approach, through a serene, tree-shaded garden and
past the Art Café and Bar, is charming. The works in
the gallery are mainly by 19th- and 20th-century
Corfiot painters and sculptors, but there are also
medieval paintings including the powerful *Decapitation
of John the Baptist* by Michael Damaskinos. Notable
Corfiot painters include Charalambos Pachis, whose
The Assassination of Capodistrias is a touch
melodramatic, but compelling. The French-influenced
painting of the Liston, *Night in Corfu* (1913), by George
Samartzis has a happy relevance for holidaymakers.
Modern works by the engraver Nikolaos Ventouras,
and later abstract paintings by Aglaia Papa, are also on
display. Next to the café-bar there is another smaller
gallery, which stages various exhibitions.

✉ Paláti tou Agíou Michaíl tou Georgíou (Palace of St Michael and St
George, East Wing), Corfu Town ⏱ Tue–Sat 8.30–3, Sun 9.30–2.30
🍴 Art Gallery Café (€€), behind the palace ♿ None 💶 Moderate
🔁 Paláti tou Agíou Michaíl tou Georgíou (➤ 41)

KATO KORAKIÁNA

In this village is the Castello Gallery, an outstation of
the Greek National Art Gallery. At nearby Evropoúli
there is a museum that celebrates the life of Corfiot
John Capodistrias, first president of the united Greek
nation.

Castello Art Gallery: ✉ Kato Korakiána ☎ (26610) 72227
⏱ Wed–Mon 9–4; also Wed & Fri 5–9. Kapodistrias Museum:
✉ Koukoristsa, near Evropoúli, 5km west of Corfu Town ☎ (26610)
39528 ⏱ Wed & Sat 11am–1pm

MOUSEÍO SOLOMOÚ (SOLOMOS MUSEUM)

The poet Dionysios Solomos (1798–1857) was born on
the island of Zakynthos but spent his later life on
Corfu. He championed the modern Greek language,
and in 1863 the first two stanzas of his 1822 poem,
'Hymn to Liberty', were set to music by his friend, the
composer Nicholas Mantzaros. The combined work
became the Greek national anthem. Goethe described
Solomos as the 'Byron of the East'. The Solomos
Museum, just off Arseniou, is a reconstruction of the
house in which Solomos lived and which was destroyed
by bombs during World War II. A visit to the museum
may prove frustrating for visitors without knowledge of
Greek, but the atmosphere alone is rewarding.

✉ 3rd Parados, Arseniou, Corfu Town ☎ (26610) 30674
⏱ Jun–Oct 9.30–2; Nov–May 9.30–1 🍴 Cafés, restaurants (€–€€)
in Old Port Square ♿ None 💶 Moderate 🔁 Byzantine Museum
(➤ 39) ❓ Labels are in Greek only

Excursions

DIAPÓNTIA NISIÁ (DIAPONDÍA ISLANDS)

Corfu's Diapondía Islands are the northwest outposts of Greece. The nearest, and smallest, of the three inhabited islands is Mathráki, just under 5km from the Corfu coast. The two others are Eríkoussa and Othoní. The Diapondías have a long history; flint tools of the early Stone Age, the neolithic and the Bronze Age have been discovered on all of them, and for centuries they were important refuges for ships. All the islands have beaches and there are some tourist services, including a few tavernas and rooms to let – but choice is very limited. Mathráki is the handsomest of the islands, deeply wooded and with a very long beach. Othoní has several beaches including Aspri Ammos, the 'white sand', on its western shore. Eríkoussa, the busiest of the three, has a long curving beach in front of its main settlement, Porto.

PAXOÍ (PAXOS)

The island, 11km long and 5km wide, is swathed in olive trees, pines and cypresses, giving the hilly interior a deceptively rounded look. It is a delightful place, where life is measured at a much slower pace than on Corfu. Dusty tracks wind through the olive groves to small settlements or to remote coves and pebble beaches – although Paxos is not a beach-lover's paradise. The south and west coasts of the island are spectacular, with steep cliffs, huge, cathedral-like sea caves and wind-sculpted rock formations. The limestone of the cliffs glows pink and ochre in the setting sun. The island's principal port, Gáïos has a lively little harbourside *plateía* with streets and alleyways radiating from it. The two other main settlements are Lákka to the north and Longos, on the east coast, midway between Gáïos and Lákka. Buses operate between all three, but exploring the island on foot is a rewarding option, although you need more than a day visit to get the best from this Ionian jewel.

ANTIPAXOÍ (ANTIPAXOS)

Antipaxos is a mere 3sq km in size; the island is a complex of tracks and paths through olive- and vine-growing country, a place where some kind of solitude can be found even in summer. The east coast beaches at Vrika, Mesovrika and Voutoumi are attractive, although they can become crowded with visitors. There are enough tavernas to cater for daytime needs.

GETTING THERE

Regular ferries operate to the Diapondía Islands and Paxos from Corfu Town and there are excursions from Sidári and Ágios Stefganos (northwest) to the Diapondía Islands daily in the summer, depending on sea conditions. The crossing to the Diapondía Islands can be choppy in the open waters. Cruise boats from Kávos go to Paxos. It is essential to make enquiries at several ferry agencies because of a complex and often changing ferry system. You can reach Antipaxos by ferry from Gáïos on Paxos.

DID YOU KNOW?

Mythical Paxos is said to have been severed from the southern tip of Corfu by one blow of the sea god Poseidon's trident. Poseidon then dragged the new island far enough south to make of it an idyllic retreat for himself and his lady, Amphitriti, thus setting a precedent for exclusiveness.

The lustrous green olive trees of Paxos, the island's main crop and concern

For Children

Corfiot children are very adept at entertaining themselves. Swimming is often second nature to local youngsters and basketball and football are Greek obsessions. In Corfu, as in all of Greece, children are well-integrated into adult society. Yours will be welcomed in tavernas where local people are happy for them to be seen and heard – within reason…

EAST COAST

Beaches on Corfu's east coast are mainly shingle and often narrow. They are usually very safe for bathing and are accessible from the main coast road. Beach equipment and watersports are available at most coastal resorts. Beaches can become very crowded. Best beaches for children include Ágios Stéfanos (Northwest) (➤ 51), Barbati (➤ 52), Dassiá (➤ 52), Kalámi (➤ 32), Messongí (➤ 53) and Moraïtika (➤ 37).

NORTH COAST

Corfu's north-coast beaches are generally much longer than their east-coast counterparts and have more sand. They tend to be narrow, but do not shelve steeply into the sea, making them safe for small children. These beaches may be affected in the afternoons by onshore winds. Beach equipment and watersports are available at most of these beaches. Best beaches for children include Acharávi (➤ 50), Róda (➤ 53) and Sidári (➤ 46).

WEST COAST

Corfu's west-coast beaches are much sandier than those on the east coast and they are often longer and wider. They are less accessible – many are reached down long, winding roads – and may be affected by wind at times. The prevailing wind in summer is known as the *maistro*; it blows from between northwest and west northwest. This makes for ideal windsurfing conditions at the two Ágios Geórgios beaches (➤ 50–51), and the beaches at Ágios Górdis (➤ 51) and Glyfáda (➤ 52–53). The *maistro* is variable in strength, but usually rises in the afternoon and drops away in the evening. A disadvantage of this breeziness, on the more open west-coast beaches, is that sand may become windblown. Most types of beach equipment and watersport are available at the more accessible and popular resorts. The best beaches for children are Ágios Geórgios (Northwest) (➤ 50), Ágios Górdis (➤ 51) and Glifida, where the beach shelves steeply in places, (➤ 52–53).

CYCLING

General advice on cycling is covered on page 20. Cycling on Corfu's public roads is not advised for very young children or for those who are inexperienced. There is, however, a vast network of off-road tracks which can be enjoyed. The best areas are in the low-lying southern part of Corfu and in the northern coastal strip behind Sidári, Róda and Acharavi. Children should not explore off-road tracks by bike on their own as they could get lost. For bike-hire outlets ➤ 82.

FESTIVALS

Local festivals (➤ 22) are excellent entertainment for children on holiday (adults too), not least because local youngsters take part wholeheartedly. There is always something going on, and even in the lulls, the Corfiots generate an atmosphere of excitement and goodwill.

GO-KARTS

There are go-kart circuits at Kanoni: Karto-Mania ☎ (26610) 43545 and Sidári: Sidári Go-Kart ☎ (26610) 99076. The suitability of these is left to parental judgement.

HORSE RIDING

There are several riding stables on Corfu. Most cater for children and a family outing on horseback can be delightful and a wonderful way to explore the island. For riding stables ➤ 83.

WATERPARKS

AQUALAND (€€€)

Corfu's water-fun park with a wide range of water-slides, swimming pools and other aquatic attractions. ✉ Ágios Ioannas (on Pélekas–Érmones road) ☎ (26610) 58351/52963; www.aqualand.com.gr 🚌 Blue bus 8 from Plateia San Rocco, Corfu Town to Aqualand 🕐 Daily May–Jun, Sep–Oct 10–6, Jul–Aug 10–7

HYDROPOLIS (€€€)

Not a patch on Aqualand, but offers waterslides, pools and pet corner. Also incorporates a sports centre with gym and tennis courts. ✉ On main road, on Kassiópi side of Acharávi ☎ (26630) 64700

WATER SLIDES

There are small water slides at Ágios Geórgios (Northwest), Moraïtika and Sidári

WATERSPORTS

Most of Corfu's popular beaches provide facilities for various watersports, ranging from waterskiing and paragliding, to pedaloes and canoes. Banana boats and ringos, which involve inflated floats being towed behind speedboats, appeal to children and young people. Banana boats are generally a safe option, but ringo-riding, in which you sit inside an inflated inner tube is a fairly robust experience and is not suited to young children. Some beaches, such as Moraïtika (➤ 37), have ringo-riding for children.

GENER...

Guard ag... ...., and sunstroke. A holiday can be ruined in the first few days from too much exposure to the sun. Take precautions by using reputable sun-screening creams and by rationing your sunbathing. Be very careful not to expose young children to the sun for long periods. There are not many sea hazards on Ionian beaches, but keep an eye out for jellyfish, and for sea urchins near rocks.

Holidaymakers relaxing on the sands of Ágios Geórgios, a resort north on the northwest coast of the island

Places to Have Lunch

BOUGAINVILEA (€€)
Corfu specialities are on offer here, in an attractive setting away from the crowds.
✉ Town Hall Square, Corfu Town ☎ (26610) 41607

CAVO BARBARO (€–€€)
Cheerful service and good traditional food at laid-back Avláki Beach. The place to come after a hard morning sun-bathing.
✉ Avláki Beach ☎ (26630) 81905

EN PLO (€€)
Marvellous venue with views across the sea to the Old Fortress, and with stylish lunch snacks.
✉ St Nikilas Gate, Faliraki, Corfu Town ☎ (26610) 81813

LA FAMIGLIA (€–€€)
Italian café-restaurant serving imaginative snacks and light meals on a busy, colourful street in Corfu Town.
✉ 30 Maniarizi Arlioti Street
☎ (26610) 30270

Coffee and pastries on a tray

GALLINI (€€)
Highly popular waterfront taverna that's good for steaks, *kheftiko* and other Greek dishes.
✉ Ágios Stéfanos
☎ (26630) 81492

GREAT SHAKES (€)
The English proprietors serve lunch, or late breakfast. Beer from the barrel, if you're missing it.
✉ Dassiá, on main road

KAFESAS (€€)
A popular fish taverna above the beach in southwest Corfu.
✉ Ágios Georgios (southwest) ☎ (26620) 51196

SEA BREEZE (€€)
Popular taverna overlooking the sea with good Corfiot cuisine and party nights.
✉ Ágios Górdis ☎ (26610) 53214

SYMPOSIUM (€€–€€€)
Well researched menu of ancient Greek cooking, beautifully presented. Also classic and unusual Corfiot and Greek dishes, plus Ina's own creations.
✉ Ágios Stéfanos (Northwest)

CORFU
where to...

Corfu Town

PRICES

Approximate prices for a full meal with a glass of wine:

€ = under €15
€€ = €15–€25
€€€ = over €25

BOOKING MEALS

Booking for town restaurants and for the more sophisticated and popular resort restaurants is advisable in high season. For most beachside and village tavernas, booking by phone is often irrelevant. The owners pack you in with gusto and good humour. If a taverna is full, extra tables and chairs may simply be added to garden, yard or village square. Squeeze in, tuck in, and enjoy…

EATING PLACES

There are some fine distinctions between eating places in Greece. An *estiatorio* is a restaurant offering international cuisine; a taverna serves traditional Greek food; a *psistaria* is a spit-roast and chargrill taverna; a *psarotaverna* is a fish taverna; a *kafenio* is a village café; a *zaharoplastio* is a café-pâtisserie. On Corfu, the difference between a restaurant and a taverna is that the former has more sophisticated service with a wider menu, and is more likely to be found in Corfu Town. Tavernas are far more informal and dominate the scene in resorts and villages.

AEGLI (€€–€€€)

A classic Liston restaurant. Eat underneath the arches or on the Esplanade, beneath the trees. Good Corfiot *tiss katsarolass* (casserole) and choice of equally tasty fish dishes.
✉ 23 Kapodistrias ☎ (26610) 31949 🕐 Lunch and dinner

ARPI (€€)

Greek country cooking comes to town – even the bread is oven-baked. Start with *fasolata* (bean soup), then try the cockerel *pastitsada*, or *soopi-ess* (cuttlefish). Good Greek Cabernet to go with it.
✉ Panayioti Giotopoulou (off Town Hall Square) ☎ (26610) 27715 🕐 Lunch and dinner

ART GALLERY CAFÉ (€€)

Pleasantly fashionable café-bar adjoining the Municipal Art Gallery. Good place to kick off an evening with drinks.
✉ Palace of St Michael and St George, East Wing, Esplanade 🕐 All day

BOUGAINVILEA (€€)

A delightful position overlooking the Square adds to the pleasing experience of this friendly, traditional restaurant that offers Corfiot specialities at their best.
✉ Town Hall Square ☎ (26610) 41607 🕐 Lunch and dinner

CAFÉ BANCA (€–€€)

Good selection of tasty snacks and range of drinks.
✉ 42b Alexandras Avenue (off San Rocco Square) ☎ (26610) 43290 🕐 All day

CAMPIELLO CRÊPERIE (€)

Good crêperie in quiet part of the Old Town. Large selection of crêpes and fine wines.
✉ 25 Petridou ☎ (26610) 23517 🕐 Dinner

CHRISOMALLIS (€)

Traditional family-run in-town taverna. Corfiot food – *pastitsada*, *stifado*, *sofrito*, *moussaká* and grilled meats. Popular with locals and excellent value.
✉ 6 Nikifourou Theotoki (behind the Liston) ☎ (26610) 30342 🕐 All day

CHRISTA'S CRÊPERIE (€)

In a great location just up from Filarmonikis. Delicious selection and intimate atmosphere.
✉ Sophocleous Dousmani ☎ (26610) 40227 🕐 Lunch and dinner. Dinner only in winter

CRÊPERIE KOUKONÁRA (€)

This busy streetside creperie offers tasty take-aways.
✉ 7 Filarmonikis ☎ (26610) 81737 🕐 All day

LA CUCINA (€€)

Italian restaurant specializing in fresh pasta with seafood, smoked salmon or prosciutto. Excellent pizzas too.
✉ 17 Guildford Street, Porta Remounda ☎ (26610) 45029 🕐 Dinner

EN PLO (€€)

Marvellous venue with views across the sea to the Old Fortress, and with stylish lunch snacks, salads, moussaka and pricier selection of meat or fish *mezes*.

✉ St Nikolas Gate, Faliraki, Corfu Town ☎ (26610) 81813 🕐 All day

LA FAMIGLIA (€)

Full-blooded Italian café-restaurant. Linguine with *vorgole* (mussels); lasagne, including a vegetarian version; canelloni; *polenta con pancetta*. Imaginative desserts.

✉ 30 Maniarizi Arlioti ☎ (26610) 30270 🕐 All day

THE FOREST (€)

Tucked away between Filarmonikis and Ágios Theodoras, this atmospheric café-bar offers tasty omelettes, sandwiches and *mezes*. Pretty garden with old oven, a well and even a pet rabbit.

✉ 3 Themistokleoys ☎ (69775) 43251 🕐 Daily 10.30–3, 6–late

IL GIARDINO (€€€)

Very classy Italian restaurant offering Tuscan cuisine and fine wines.

✉ 4b Vraila. Opposite the Archaeological Museum ☎ (26610) 30723 🕐 Dinner

KOCHLIAS (€€)

Bar-café serving coffees, fruit juices, ouzo, wines, beers, *mezes*, sandwiches and ice-cream.

✉ The Liston ☎ (26610) 28188 🕐 All day

MOURAGIO (€–€€)

Down-to-earth place offering reasonably priced local dishes and a great variety of *mezes*.

✉ 15 Arseniou Street ☎ (26610) 33815 🕐 Lunch and dinner

OLD FORTRESS CAFÉ (€)

At the top of the Old Fortress, with fine views of Garítsa Bay. Pastas and salads served all day. Popular spot by night.

✉ Old Fortress, Spianáda (Esplanade) ☎ (26610) 48550 🕐 Daily 9AM–2AM

PORTA REMOUNDA (€€–€€)

Very good *psarotaverna* (fish taverna). Try *bourdeto*, a variety of small fish in a rich tomato-based sauce; or *soopi-ess* (cuttlefish).

✉ 14 Moustoxidi Street, off Kapodistrias ☎ (26610) 48661 🕐 Lunch and dinner

REX (€€–€€€)

Behind the Liston, a long-established popular restaurant. Adventurous sauces, including a local speciality, chicken in kumquat sauce. Good selection of Greek wines.

✉ 66 Kapodistrias ☎ (26610) 39649 🕐 Lunch and dinner

TO DIMARCHIO (€€–€€€)

Excellent mix of Greek and international cuisine and a lovely setting make this restaurant popular with locals and visitors alike.

✉ Plateia Dimarcheio ☎ (26610) 39031 🕐 Lunch and dinner

VENETIAN WELL (€€–€€€)

At the Italianate heart of the Old Town. The remarkable menu spans East and West plus Greek specialities and delicious home-made desserts.

✉ Kremásti Square ☎ (26610) 44761 🕐 Lunch and dinner. Closed Sun

VEGETARIAN OPTIONS

Vegetarians may have difficulty in finding non-meat dishes in traditional tavernas. But, as so many *mezes* (starters) are vegetable only, you can often make a meal of them alone. Try *spanokeftedes* (spinach balls), *manitaria* (mushrooms), *dolmadakia* (vine leaves stuffed with rice), *saganaki* cheese fried in oil, and feta cheese. Be careful with 'mixed' dishes such as pasta with vegetables, or vegetable casserole, as small pieces of meat are often mixed in regardless.

Around the Island

COFFEE

The Greeks know well that coffee-drinking makes philosophers or gossips of us all. For the safe, familiar stuff, 'Nescafé' is universally recognised as meaning instant coffee. Try *kafes Ellenika*, Greek coffee, made from thick grounds, served in tiny cups, either *sketo* (unsweetened), *metrio* (medium sweet), or *gliko* (sweetened). Do not swallow in one gulp. Sip gently. It comes with a glass of water, which can be added in small portions to settle the grounds. Try too, *kafes frappe*, a long glass of smooth, iced coffee, sweetened or unsweetened, again accompanied by a glass of water.

ACHARÁVI

MAISTRO (€–€€)
A lovely beachside setting for a wide-ranging traditional menu offering fish specialities, local Corfiot dishes and crêpes.
✉ Overlooking the middle of the beach ☎ (26630) 63020
🕐 Lunch and dinner

THE PUMP HOUSE (€–€€)
This well-run place offers tasty Corfiot specialities and has an excellent fresh fish and seafood menu.
✉ Main Street ☎ (26630) 63271 🕐 Lunch and dinner

ÁGIOS GEÓRGIOS (SOUTHWEST)

KAFESAS (€€)
A popular fish taverna above the beach in southwest Corfu. If you don't fancy a main dish, try the delicious fish *mezes*.
✉ Above beach ☎ (26620) 51196 🕐 Lunch and dinner

RESTAURANT PANORAMA (€€)
Friendly family staff serve up excellent Greek specialities, including surely one of the best *kleftiko* (baked lamb) you'll ever taste.
✉ At the coast near the centre of the resort ☎ (26620) 52352 🕐 Lunch and dinner

ÁGIOS GÓRDIS

SEA BREEZE (€€)
In a lovely location with terraces overlooking the beach. Features regular Greek nights including music, dancers and jugglers. There is a play area for children and a good fun atmosphere.
✉ Towards the southern end of the beach ☎ (26610) 53214 🕐 Lunch and dinner

ÁGIOS STÉFANOS (NORTHEAST)

EUCALYPTUS (€€)
Beside the shingle beach, the Eucalyptus offers good international cuisine in a great setting.
✉ On the north side of the bay where the approach road turns south ☎ (26630) 82007 🕐 Lunch and dinner

ÁGIOS STÉFANOS (NORTHWEST)

TAVERNA O MANTHOS (€–€€)
Dine out overlooking the beach from the garden restaurant. Corfiot specialities and barbecue food.
✉ At the north end of the seafront near the jetty ☎ (26630) 51066 🕐 Lunch and dinner

AGNI

TAVERNA AGNI (€€–€€€)
Popular and friendly beachside eating place, family run (Corfiot and English) and with marvellous local cuisine. Try anchovy fillets marinated in herb-infused olive oil and aubergine slices rolled round feta cheese and baked in a tasty sauce. Main dishes include lamb casseroled in red wine and chicken cooked in champagne.
✉ Overlooking Agni beach ☎ (26630) 91142 🕐 Lunch and dinner

TAVERNA NIKOLAS (€€–€€€)

The most traditional of Agni's beach tavernas, set up over 35 years ago. It has a picturesque location, and with its very relaxing atmosphere and good Greek food is popular with English tourists. Greek dancing some evenings.

✉ On the beach ☎ (26630) 91243 🕐 Lunch and dinner

TOULA'S (€€–€€€)

Yet another first-class taverna at Agni. Beach-side eating with classic fish dishes as well as meat. Try fish *mezes* for starters, including anchovies marinated in vinegar and lemon juice. Follow with prawn pilaff.

✉ Overlooks beach at road end ☎ (26630) 91350 🕐 Lunch and dinner

ALONÁKI

ALONÁKI BAY TAVERNA (€)

One of the most attractive and popular west-coast tavernas. Homely, with tree-shaded views to the sea. Good Corfiot home cooking, fresh fish and potent local wine.

✉ Just north of Lake Korissión, on a rough track ☎ (26610) 75872/76118 🕐 Lunch and dinner

ÁNO KORAKIÁNA

TAVERNA LUNA D'ARGENTO (€€)

Popular all-in experience, with great traditional food accompanied by Greek dancing and – a splash of exotica – belly dancing.

✉ In village ☎ (26630) 22531 (booking advised) 🕐 Dinner

AVLÁKI

CAVO BARBARO (€–€€)

Cheerful service and good traditional food at laid-back Avláki Beach. This is old-style Corfiot cooking at its best with fish and meat dishes and treats such as onion pie.

✉ Avláki Beach ☎ (26630) 81905 🕐 Lunch and dinner

BENÍTSES

PAXINOS (€€)

Traditional Corfiot casserole dishes and locally caught fish. Popular with locals.

✉ Harbour Square in the old village ☎ (26610) 72339 🕐 Lunch and dinner

DOUKÁDES

ELIZABETH'S (€)

Elisabeth's is a Corfiot institution that manages to retain its village taverna atmosphere and its authentic dishes such as *pastitsada* (beef or cockerel in a spicy tomato stew, with macaroni).

✉ Main Street ☎ (26630) 41728 🕐 Lunch and dinner

ÉRMONES

NAUSIKA RESTAURANT BAR (€–€€)

It you like eating while looking at a great sunset this is the place, plus excellent traditional food and live music.

✉ On south side of river, overlooking beach 🕐 Lunch and dinner

NON-ALCOHOLIC DRINKS

You can certainly ask for tea (*tsa-i*), but try breaking the habit of a lifetime. If tea is available, make it clear if you want milk (*gala*), or sugar (*zahari*), with it. Orange juice in the best cafés is made from fresh oranges, and is delicious. Soft drinks (*anapsiktika*), are available in universal brands. Greek soft drinks, such as *portokalada* (fizzy orange), and lemon-flavoured *lemonada* are very sweet.

GINGER BEER

Ginger beer, or *tsin tsin birra*, to give it the proper Corfiot name, is still available on Corfu and can be bought in the Liston cafés. A legacy of the British protectorate, the drink is made in traditional fashion using the finest ingredients of grated ginger, lemon juice, lemon oil, water and sugar. The mix is brewed in large cauldrons and is best taken fresh, although, traditionally, it was stored for long periods in stone bottles that were sealed with little glass marble stoppers and kept in the cool waters of island wells.

GLYFÁDA

ALOHA BEACH BAR (€)

More of a music bar but with a restaurant offering breakfast, lunch and *mezes* in the evening.

✉ Immediately south of entrance to beach ☎ (26610) 94380 🕓 10AM until late

GOUVIÁ

ARGO (€€€)

Join the yachting crowd at this pleasant modern restaurant at Gouviá Marina. There's a relaxing ambience in which to enjoy well-prepared fish dishes and other treats on the international menu.

✉ Gouviá Marina ☎ (26610) 99251 🕓 Lunch and dinner

GORGONA (€€–€€€)

You won't get *gorgona* (mermaid) on a platter at this terrific fish taverna, but the great selection of fresh fish and seafood and the palette of sauces is unbeatable.

✉ Main Street ☎ (26610) 90261 🕓 Apr–Oct daily, weekends rest of year

IPSOS (ÝPOS)

VICEROY INDIAN (€–€€)

The first Indian restaurant on Corfu. Very authentic, with wide-ranging menu and proper Tandoori oven-cooking.

✉ At north end of resort, near turn off to old Venetian boatyard ☎ (26610) 93814 🕓 Dinner. Closed Mon

KALÁMI

PEPES TAVERNA (€€)

Pepes is a traditional, family-run taverna offering good Corfiot and fresh fish dishes. Greek dancing at weekends.

✉ At centre of village ☎ (26630) 91180 🕓 Lunch and dinner

THE WHITE HOUSE (€€)

Popular for fish, sea views and literary connections: Lawrence Durrell lived here (1937–38) and wrote his pastoral idyll, *Prospero's Cell*.

✉ On south side of the bay ☎ (26630) 91251 🕓 Lunch and dinner

KANÓNI

CAPTAIN'S (€–€€)

Old-time favourite, with friendly owner 'Captain' George. Authentic Greek dishes are served with flair; generous helpings. Try the *kopanisti* (peppered cheese) and the *gigantes* (beans in sauce). Good *pastitsada* and *souvlaki*.

✉ Just past the viewpoint area ☎ (26610) 40502 🕓 All day

NAFSIKA (€€)

Classy food, from lavish Greek dishes to chicken curry or pork fillet with mustard. Equally lavish desserts include chocolate mousse and cheesecake, as well as Greek favourites such as *baklava* and *kataifi*. Good wine list.

✉ 11 Nafsikas, opposite Divani Hotel ☎ (26610) 44354 🕓 Dinner

KASSIÓPI

LITTLE ITALY (€€)

The southern Italian pasta and risotto at this pleasant

and popular restaurant are at the very top of the Kassiópi menu.
✉ Kassiópi ☎ (26630) 81749
🕐 Lunch and dinner

PETRINO'S (€€)

Located on the exit road from the village's central square, this excellent taverna and wine bar offers the best of traditional and international cuisine.
✉ Kassiópi ☎ (26630) 81760
🕐 Lunch and dinner

KATO KORAKIÁNA

ETRUSCO (€€€)

Svelte interiors add to the sophisticated appeal of this fine restaurant where international cuisine with Italian influences is the style. Meat and fish are lovingly and subtly prepared. Booking is advised.
✉ Kato Korakána ☎ (26610) 93342 🕐 Dinner

KÁVOS

PUFF THE MAGIC DRAGON (€–€€)

There are good helpings of well-prepared Chinese and Indian food under the same roof at this cheerful restaurant at the heart of Kávos.
✉ Kávos ☎ (26620) 61146
🕐 Lunch and dinner

THE DRUNKEN SQUID (€–€€)

Next to Puff The Magic Dragon and run by the same team, this Tex-Mex eatery masquerades as a Wild West fort, complete with working draw bridge. Very big servings of steaks

and Mexican dishes are the order of the day.
✉ Kávos ☎ (26620) 61192
🕐 Lunch and dinner

KINOPIASTES

TRIPA TAVERNA (€€)

Popular venue where famous past guests include François Mitterrand, Aristotle Onassis and Jane Fonda, though not necessarily together. There's a set menu and plent of it; from delicious *mezes* to all the Corfiot favourites. Music and Greek dancing add to the fun. Booking advised.
✉ Village is just off road from Corfu Town to Sinarádes
☎ (26610) 56333 🕐 Dinner

KONTÓKALI (KONDOKALI)

GEREKOS (€€€)

This top-of-the-range, yet intimate, restaurant prepares delicious dishes including Italian-influenced fish stews as well as char-grilled fish.
✉ Kondókali ☎ (26610) 91281 🕐 Lunch and dinner

LÁKONES

GOLDEN FOX (€€)

Stunning setting with views down to the coast. International menu, snack bar and pool.
✉ On the road to Makrádes
☎ (26630) 49101/2
🕐 Lunch and dinner

LIPÁDES

CRICKETER (€–€€)

Reliable traditional fare, including Corfiot specialities, are served up

FAST FOOD

Fast food in Greece is quickly becoming internationalised. *Tost* (toasted sandwiches with savoury fillings) are very popular, as are pizzas and hamburgers. But try *tiropita* (cheese pie, sometimes with egg), and *spanakopita* (spinach pie). When prepared well they are delicious, and addictive. *Gyros* are Greek versions of fast-food shops, where large rounds of meat are grilled on revolving 'gyros'. The result is tasty kebabs and garnish, in pita bread.

WINES

Greek wines are often dismissed, but they have kept the Greeks smiling and singing for a long time. As long as you are not an ostentatious cork-sniffer, you'll find some good wines on Corfu. These include Santa Domenica, light white and red, made from *kakotrygis* grapes. Some tavernas make their own wine, *varelisio*, from the barrel and this can be extremely good. Corfu's most famous wine is the expensive and elusive Theotoki Roppa. Retsina is a good standby. This resinated wine, common throughout Greece is an acquired taste, but when it is good and from the barrel, it is persuasive; when it is bad, usually from the bottle, it can be wicked.

at this long-established taverna where you dine surrounded by a gallery of Corfu's cricketing history. Good local wine and locally sourced produce.
✉ Elli Beach ☎ (26630) 41295 ⏱ Lunch and dinner

PALAIOKASTRÍTSA (PALEOKASTRITSA)

THE ROCK (€–€€)

The terrace of this popular restaurant, *Bráxos* (the rock) is on a rocky outcrop overlooking the sea. Traditional Corfiot dishes are well-prepared and tasty.
✉ Harbour, Paleokastritsa ☎ (26630) 41128/41233 ⏱ Lunch and dinner

PAXOÍ (PAXOS)

LA ROSA DI PAXOS (€€)

Mihales Dahetos and his Italian wife run this delightful restaurant overlooking Lákka harbour. Choose from Greek and Italian dishes, and fresh fish cooked with herbs. Good choice of wines including a strong white from the family vineyard in Antipaxos. Book in high season.
✉ Lákka ☎ (26620) 31470 ⏱ Lunch and dinner

PÉLEKAS

JIMMY'S (€€)

Jimmy and his family have been serving traditional Corfiot food here for over 25 years. It's a cheerful place and there are nicely furnished rooms with fine views if you want to stay.
✉ Pélekas village ☎ (26610) 94284 ⏱ Lunch and dinner

SUNSET RESTAURANT (€€–€€€)

High living at a high level. Eat on the terrace of this stylish hotel while the sun sets. Mediterranean cuisine to suit all tastes.
✉ By Kaiser's Lookout ☎ (26610) 94230 ⏱ Lunch and dinner

SÍDARI

MIKEY'S INN (€–€€)

A cheerful, upbeat British-style bar and eatery, Mikey's offers grills, curries, salads and much more. There's a friendly welcome for families.
✉ Main Street ☎ (26630) 95140 ⏱ All day until late

VIROS

LE GRAND BALCON (€–€€)

Despite the name, this place serves up all Greek food from a huge menu. Situated in a remarkable position with views across Ipsos Bay. Reached from the Spartýlas road, or from the main coast road through a little gate, then up steep steps.
✉ On first hairpin bend of Spartýlas road above coast road junction ☎ (26610) 93958 ⏱ Dinner

STAMATIS (€)

Popular and very friendly taverna. Should not be missed. Superb Corfiot food, *mezes* are a feast in themselves. Great house wine and impromptu music. Reservations are advised.
✉ Viros (near Vrioni) ☎ (26610) 39249 ⏱ Dinner. Closed Sun

Corfu Town

ARCADION (€€€)

A 1960s building with a Venetian façade; fine position overlooking the end of the Liston and across to the Old Fortress. The Arcadion has had a thorough upgrade; as have its prices.

✉ 44 Kapodistriou ☎ (26610) 37670; www.arcadionhotel.com ⏰ All year

ATLANTIS (€€)

Modern hotel at New Port, overlooking busy Xenofondos Stratigou Street. Several minutes' walk to town centre. Reasonable rooms. Very good restaurant and bar with impeccable service.

✉ 48 Xenofondos Stratigou ☎ (26610) 35560; email: atlanker@mail.otenet.gr ⏰ All year

BELLA VENEZIA (€€–€€€)

Stylish hotel in refurbished classical mansion. Charming gardens and a pavilion breakfast room and restaurant. In a quiet street close to centre.

✉ 4 N Zambeli ☎ (26610) 46500; email: belvenht@hol.gr ⏰ Open all year

BRETAGNE (€€)

Well-appointed modern hotel on the southern outskirts of Corfu Town. Close to the airport so it suffers some noise.

✉ 27 Georgaki Ethnicou Stadiou, Garitsa ☎ (26610) 30724/35690; email: brhotel@otenet.gr ⏰ All year

CAVALIERI (€€€)

In a beautifully reconstructed Venetian building at the quiet end of the Esplanade. The rooftop bar, open to non-residents, has marvellous evening ambience.

✉ 4 Kapodistriou ☎ (26610) 39041/39336; fax (26610) 39283; www.cavalieri-hotel.com ⏰ All year

CORFU PALACE (€€€)

Top luxury hotel overlooking Garitsa Bay. Beautiful gardens, sun terraces and pools. Haute cuisine restaurant and in-house entertainment.

✉ 2 Leoforos Dimokratias ☎ (26610) 39485/39487; fax (26610) 31749; www.corfu palace.com ⏰ Apr–Oct

HOTEL KONSTAN-TINOUPOLIS (€€)

This fine old building at the heart of the Old Port has nicely renovated rooms. Friendly service.

✉ 11 K Zavitsianoy Street ☎ (26610) 48716–8; www.konstantinouplis.co,.gr ⏰ All year

PALACE MON REPOS (€€€)

A fairly swish renovation has resulted in a classical makeover for this well-positioned Garitsa hotel. There's a restaurant and outdoor pool. It's about a 2km walk along the seafront into town.

✉ Garitsa Bay ☎ (26610) 32783 ⏰ All year

PHOENIX (€)

One of the town's few cheaper options, this pleasant, low-key hotel is near the airport, but is 1km into town.

✉ 2 Chris. Smyrnis, Garista ☎ (26610) 42290 ⏰ All year

PRICES

Approximate price for a double room for one night. (Prices are for the room, not per person.)

€ = under €60
€€ = €60–€100
€€€ = over €100

CHECKING IN AND OUT

Hotel reception will ask for your passport on registering. It should be returned to you immediately the details have been recorded. Most hotels in the upper grades accept payment by credit card. Smaller, lower-grade hotels usually prefer cash. In Corfu Town there are a number of 24-hour cash-points from which money can be withdrawn.

Around the Island

SECURITY AND SAFETY

Greek people are noted for their honesty. Reputable hotels are generally secure and most have a safe area for small items of value.

Most hotel lifts in Greece do not have cabin doors and the passing shaft wall is unguarded. Children, especially, should take great care.

ACHARÁVI

ACHARÁVI BEACH HOTEL (€€)
Small, beach-side hotel with its own pool, tennis, sports and restaurant.
✉ Overlooking beach
☎ (26630) 63102/63124; fax (26630) 63461; email: achbht @otenet.gr ◷ May–Oct

IONIAN PRINCESS (€€)
Sizeable, modern hotel a few minutes from the beach, with gardens, pool, children's pool and playground, tennis and restaurant.
✉ Between main road and beach ☎ (26630) 63135; fax (26630) 63111; www.ionian princess.gr ◷ May–Oct

ÁGIOS GEÓRGIOS (SOUTHWEST)

GOLDEN SANDS HOTEL (€)
Looks towards the sea. Handsome little church opposite in big open area adds a sense of space. The hotel has a swimming pool, children's play area, restaurant and bar.
✉ Centre of resort ☎ (26620) 51225; fax (26620) 51140 ◷ Apr–Oct

VILLA MARGARITA (€€)
These attractive, bright two-room apartments are well appointed. There are pleasant gardens.
✉ Ágios Geórgios ☎ (26620) 51190 ◷ Apr–Oct

ÁGIOS GÓRDIS

AYIOS GORDIOS HOTEL (€–€€)
Set below spectacular mountains in its own gardens. Beach access, pool, tennis court, games.
✉ Overlooking beach
☎ (26610) 53320/53322; fax (26610) 52234; email: rizoresorts@ sympria.com
◷ Apr–Oct

ÁKROTÍRIO KOMMÉNO (CAPE KOMMÉNO)

GRECOTEL CORFU IMPERIAL (€€€)
Luxury hotel with sea views and set amid landscaped gardens. Large pool, tennis courts, boutiques, beauty salon, restaurants, bars and private beaches.
✉ Komméno–Gouviá
☎ (26610) 8840; www.grecotel.gr ◷ Apr–Oct

ALYKÉS

IBEROSTAR KERKYRA GOLF (€€€)
Large, modern hotel offering numerous facilities, including pools, watersports, tennis, beach area, restaurants, bars and nightclub.
✉ On main road, 3km north of Corfu Town centre ☎ (26610) 24030; fax (26610) 24080; www.louishotels.com
◷ May–Oct

ASTRAKERI

ELENI'S (€)
Located at the charming seaward end of a quiet side road, these apartments are ideal if you have transport. The nearby Astrakeri Beach is good for youngsters. The family-owners have other apartments in the immediate area.

⊠ Astrakeri ☎ (69362)
09793/(60141) 80147
🕔 May–Oct

AVLÁKI

BOUNIAS APARTMENTS/VILLA ALEXANDRA (€–€€)

There's unbeatable value and quality at these lovely rooms and apartments that have a peaceful location, within minutes of Avláki Beach and about 2km from Kassiópi. The welcome is charming.
☎ (26630) 81183/(26610) 24333 🕔 Apr–Oct

BENÍTSES

LOUIS REGENCY (€€€)

Big hotel south of Benítses. Extensive sports facilities and access to beach below road. Beach-side taverna as well as restaurant.
⊠ South of Benítses
☎ (26610) 71211/7;
fax (26610) 71219; www.
louishotels.com 🕔 Apr–Oct

SAN STEFANO (€€–€€€)

Modern hotel and apartments in a good position above resort. Large pool, tennis courts, children's playground, restaurants, bars and shops. Courtesy bus to and from Benítses beach.
⊠ Above Benítses ☎ (26610) 71112/8; fax (26610) 72272; email: sanstefano@hol.gr
🕔 Apr–Oct

DASIÁ (DASSIÁ)

CORFU CHANDRIS HOTEL/DASSIÁ CHANDRIS HOTEL (€€€)

Two luxury, adjacent hotels under the same management. All modern amenities and direct access to beach. Pools, children's play area, tennis courts, all watersports. Restaurants, bars, shops, in-house entertainment. Courtesy bus to and from Corfu Town.
⊠ Dassiá–Káto Koriakíana
☎ Corfu Chandris/Dassiá Chandris (26610) 97100/4;fax (26610) 93458; www.chandris.gr
🕔 Apr–Oct

ELEA BEACH (€€€)

Large, modern hotel with own beachfront and gardens. All amenities, including nearby watersports centre.
⊠ Dassiá–Káto Korakíana
☎ (26610) 93490/3;
fax (26610) 93494; www.elea-beach.com 🕔 Apr–Oct

ÉRMONES

SUNMAROTEL ÉRMONES BEACH (€€€)

Bungalow-style accommo-dation on terraced hillside with stairway or funicular ride to beach. Pools, gym, tennis courts and all types of watersports. In-house entertainment, restaurant, bars.
⊠ Overlooks beach
☎ (26610) 94241; fax (26610) 94248; www.sunmarotel ermones.gr 🕔 Apr–Oct

GLYFÁDA (GLIFADA)

GLYFÁDA BEACH (€€)

Small, family-run hotel with basic but good facilities and not far from the beach.
⊠ North end of resort ☎ and fax (26610) 94257/8
🕔 Apr–Oct

71

BREAKFAST

The price of breakfast may or may not be included in the price of a room. Check details on registration. Hotel breakfasts can vary from rather dry affairs of croissants, rolls, bread, cake and jam, to a tasty selection of fruit juice, yoghurt, peaches, cereal, cold ham, cheese and boiled eggs. Coffee or tea is always served. Cooked breakfasts are available at some cafés and snack bars in many resorts.

LOUIS GRAND HOTEL (€€€)

Large and luxurious hotel. Gardens and beach access. Tennis and a range of watersports. Restaurants, bars, shops.

✉ South end of beach
☎ (26610) 94140–5;
www.louishotels.com ⊙ Apr–Oct

GOUVIÁ

LOUIS CORCYRA (€€€)

Smart luxury hotel with fine gardens and beach access. Numerous amenities, including tennis, squash, volleyball, games and a pool.

✉ Beachside location
☎ (26610) 90196; fax (26610) 91591; www.louishotels.com
⊙ Apr–Oct

PARK (€–€€)

Large, modern hotel in secluded wooded area. Good amenities include a swimming pool, tennis and volleyball. Ten minutes' walk to beach.

✉ Outskirts of resort
☎ (26610) 91347/91310; fax (26610) 91531; www.parkhotel-corfu.com ⊙ Apr–Oct

IPSOS (ÝPSOS)

ÝPSOS BEACH (€€)

Off main road, but within a few minutes of the beach. Swimming pool, restaurant and in-house entertainment.

✉ Outskirts of resort
☎ (26610) 93232; fax (26610) 93147 ⊙ Apr–Oct

KANÓNI

CORFU DIVANI PALACE (€€€)

Modern luxury hotel with gardens, sun terrace and swimming pool.

✉ 20 Nafsikas ☎ (26610) 38996; www.divanis.gr
⊙ Apr–Oct

KATO KORAKIÁNA

ETRUSCO APARTMENTS (€€)

Run by the restaurant owners of same name, these reasonable apartments are well placed for Corfu Town and nearby beaches.

✉ Kato Korakiána ☎ (26610) 93342 ⊙ Apr–Oct

KÁVOS

SAN MARINA (€€)

Alongside narrow beach but some distance from the centre. Swimming pool and watersports, and other activities organised.

✉ South end of resort
☎ (26620) 61345/6
⊙ May–Oct

KONTÓKALI (KONDÓKALI)

KONTÓKALI BAY (€€€)

Luxury hotel in gardens, with additional bungalow accommodation. Pools, entertainment and watersports, children's club, tennis courts.

✉ On peninsula by beaches
☎ (26610) 99000/2; fax (26610) 91901; www.konto kalibay.com ⊙ Apr–Oct

MESONGÍ (MESSONGÍ)

APOLLO PALACE (€€)

Quality hotel with many facilities, including pool, tennis, basketball and volleyball.

✉ Behind resort ☎ (26610) 75433/75035; fax (26610) 75602 ⏰ Apr–Oct

CHRISTINA (€–€€)

Attractive beachside hotel with restaurant and well-equipped rooms.
☎ (26610) 55294; www.hotel christina.gr ⏰ May–Oct

LÁKONES

GOLDEN FOX (€€)

You won't go short of eating opportunities at these fine apartments adjoining the Golden Fox restaurant. There are great views from front rooms and 10 per cent discount on food at the restaurant.
☎ (26630) 49101/2; www.corfu goldenfox.com ⏰ May–Oct

MORAÏTIKA

ALBATROS (€–€€)

Close to beach and a few minutes from main street. Pools in surrounding gardens.
☎ (26610) 75315/75317; fax (26610) 75484 ⏰ Apr–Oct

MIRAMARE BEACH (€€–€€€)

Luxury hotel fronted by narrow beach. Gardens lead to beachside bar. Tennis courts. Courtesy bus to Corfu Town.
☎ (26610) 75224/75226; fax (26610) 75305; www.miramarebeach.gr ⏰ May–Oct

NISÁKI

NISSAKI BEACH HOTEL (€€–€€€)

Luxury hotel in a prime coastal position. Pool, tennis courts; even crazy golf. Exclusive beach area below has all watersports and amenities, including beachside taverna.
☎ (26630) 91232/91233; fax (26630) 22079; email: nissaki@otenet.gr ⏰ Apr–Oct

PALAIOKASTRÍTSA (PALEOKASTRITSA)

AKROTIRI BEACH (€€–€€€)

In a spectacular setting on the neck of a wooded peninsula directly above the beach. All the usual amenities, including a swimming pool.
☎ (26630) 41237; fax (26630) 41277; email: belunht@hol.gr ⏰ Apr–Oct

HOTEL ODYSSEUS (€–€€)

Bright and clean rooms are on offer at this friendly place that also offers great views and a pleasant garden and pool.
☎ (26630) 41209; fax (26630) 41342 ⏰ May–mid-Oct

ZEPHYROS (€€)

Pleasant and comfortable amenities, near beach.
☎ and fax (26630) 41244 ⏰ Apr–Oct

PAXOÍ (PAXOS)

MARY'S APARTMENTS (€€–€€€)

Charming apartments in a good location over-looking the sea and not far from the main port.
☎ and fax (26620) 32205 ⏰ May–Oct

PAXOS CLUB (€€€)

Luxury hotel with some apartments. Big swimming

CAMPING

Unofficial camping is illegal in Greece. There are a number of official campsites on Corfu, although, in the way of things, they may come and go. There are reputable campsites at the following resorts:

Corfu Camping
✉ Ýpsos (Ipsos)
☎ (26610) 93246
⏰ Seasonal

Dionysus Camping Village
✉ Dafnila/Dassiá
☎ (26610) 91417;
www.dionysuscamping.gr
⏰ Seasonal

Paleokastritsa Camping
✉ Paleokastritsa
☎ (26630) 41204
⏰ Seasonal

PARKING

Local people are experts at casual parking but you are not advised to copy them. Corfu Town has convenient official parking areas in Old Port Square and on the Spianáda (Esplanade). Parking areas usually have an attendant who will issue a parking card. By the New Fortress there is a small parking area, reached from Xenefondos Stratigou by turning right up Lohagou Spyrou Vaikou Street alongside the west wall of the New Fortress.

pool, restaurant and bar. In-house entertainment.
✉ About 2km outside Gáïos
☎ (26620) 32450
🕐 May–Sep

SAN GIORGIO ROOMS (€)

Located between the New Port and Gáïos and only minutes from the town centre, these fine rooms and self-catering studios have great views and are kept to a very good standard.
✉ New Port, Gáïos
☎ (26620) 32450
🕐 May–Oct

PÉLEKAS

LEVANT (€€)

Peaceful hotel in hilltop setting. Restaurant, pool and terrace from which to enjoy the sunset extravaganza.
☎ (26610) 94230; fax (26610) 94115; www.levanthotel.com
🕐 Apr–Nov

VILLA MYRTO (€–€€)

Located near the lovely Myrtiótissa Beach these bright, nicely furnished self-catering rooms are well run and there's a friendly and very sociable welcome.
☎ (26610) 95082; www.villamyrto.com 🕐 Mar–Nov

PÉRAMA

AELOS BEACH (€€)

Very large hotel on hillside above Pérama. Several minutes to beach and to resort itself. Numerous in-house amenities include swimming pool, sun terrace and poolside bar. Children's play area.

Watersports organised at beach. Pets allowed.
☎ (26610) 33132/6; fax (26610) 40420 🕐 Apr–Oct

ALEXANDROS (€€–€€€)

Situated at heart of resort a few minutes from shingle beach. There is a swimming pool in quiet gardens with attendant taverna. Watersports and other activities organised.
☎ (26610) 36855/6; fax (26610) 33160 🕐 Apr–Oct

PÉRAMA (€)

A small hotel on main road through resort. Although the amenities are basic it is close to the beach, which makes it attractive.
☎ (26610) 33167; fax (26610) 40880 🕐 Apr–Oct

RÓDA

RÓDA VILLAGE BEACH (€€)

Very large hotel with extra bungalow accommodation. Swimming pools, children's pool area, sun terrace, tennis court. Set in large gardens with access to the beach.
☎ (26630) 64181/5; fax (26630) 63436; email: rodabeachvillage@in.gr
🕐 Apr–Sep

SIDÁRI

ALKYON HOTEL (€–€€)

Rooms are simple and on the small side at this popular hotel, but the service is excellent and friendly and the décor is fresh and bright. Meals are well prepared.
☎ (26630) 95300; www.sidarialkyon.com
🕐 Apr–Sep

Corfu Town

Corfu Town is the main all-year-round shopping centre of the island. It has all the general outlets you would expect to find in a comparable urban centre, from hardware shops to food and drink suppliers, from fashion and clothes shops to the *periptero* kiosks which sell everything from newspapers and cigarettes, to sweets and soft drinks, soap and condoms. There are some excellent wine and spirit stores and many mouth-watering *zaharoplastios*, shops that specialise in cakes, pastries and sweets. Specialities to look out for on Corfu include perishables, such as olives, herbs, spices, nuts, and cheeses like the soft white feta, made from goat and sheep milk. Virgin olive oil can be bought in supermarkets as well as in delicatessens. A drink special to the island is Kumquat (see panel ► 78).

BOOKS, NEWSPAPERS AND MAGAZINES

KIOSK

A newspaper and magazine shop behind the Liston with an astonishing international selection from fashion magazines to hobbies.
✉ 11 Kapodistrias (behind the Liston). Also at Old Port
☎ (26610) 42760

LEON MARKOSIAN

An excellent small newsagent and bookseller that sells international newspapers and a good range of books, including guidebooks, in various languages.
✉ 20 G Theotoki ☎ (26610) 39761

PLOU BOOKSHOP

A Corfu institution, worth visiting for its timeless ambience. Most books are in Greek, but there are always a few English language gems, usually about the island or cooking, to search out.
✉ 2 Parados Nikifolou Theotoki 14 (up narrow alleyway)
☎ (26610) 42128

CLOTHING, ACCESSORIES AND COSMETICS

BACKCOVER

Quality casual wear and swimwear. Top brand names include French Connection, Calvin Klein and Henri Lloyd.
✉ 51/53 N Theotoki
☎ (26610) 26735

THE BEAUTY SHOP

Cosmetics and perfumes by names such as Revlon and Estée Lauder. Also Marks & Spencer underwear.
✉ G Theotoki and Alexandras Avenue ☎ (26610) 21165

BODY SHOP

Same range as carried by Body Shop internationally. English-speaking staff.
✉ St Spyridon's Square (Plateia Iroon Kypriakou Agonos)

ENGLISH IMPORTS

Range of clothing and household goods, some non-perishable food items, English newspapers and books. Friendly staff.
✉ 1st Parados Mitropoliti

BARGAINING

Greece takes the middle ground between the western culture of fixed-price shopping and oriental bargaining, or 'haggling'. Greeks love a good haggle and so should you. Although fixed-priced shopping is the norm, especially in Corfu Town, where brand-name shops and speciality shops predominate, you may still get a flavour of bargaining at local markets. Try also the side-street shops bedecked with clothes, rugs and general goods and the roadside stalls of places such as Makrádes (► 55) on the northwest coast. It is only really acceptable to haggle over non-perishable goods.

75

PUBLIC TOILETS

There are very few public toilets in Corfu. Tavernas and restaurants must have toilets by law. The Greek for 'Gents' is *andron*, and for 'Ladies' is *gynaikon*. Public toilets may not have toilet paper available.

PUBLIC TOILETS IN CORFU TOWN

✉ Kapodistrias Street (on southern half of the Esplanade). Facility for disabled

✉ San Rocco Square. At west end, down steps. Not always at their best. Brace yourself...

In Greece, the circumference of waste pipes is small and outlets are easily blocked by toilet paper. However fastidious you may be, you should comply with local custom and dispose of toilet paper in the receptacles supplied in accommodation, restaurants, tavernas and bars, entertainment premises and public toilets.

Methodiou (on corner with San Rocco Square, signposted down alleyway) ☎ (06610) 47692

GEORGIOS N KRITIKOS

This friendly shop sells every kind of scarf, hat, cap, bag you could want, plus fabrics and dresses.
✉ 42 G Theotoki
☎ (26610) 37410

KANNABISHOP

Amazing products in this fascinating shop include clothing, shoes, cosmetics, beer, skateboards and much more, all made from cannabis hemp, and perfectly legal.
✉ 46 Kalochairetou Street
☎ (26610) 82175

MARKS & SPENCER

This famous high-street name occupies what was once the biggest cinema in town.
✉ 15–17 G Theotoki
☎ (26610) 82175

PRAXIS

Always popular with the young. Levi jeans and casual wear by O'Neill and Diesel.
✉ N Theotoki

TRIFOUNA VOULA

There's a wonderful collection of linen and lacework in this charming little shop.
✉ 21 Filarmonikis
☎ (26610) 22574

CRAFTS, ANTIQUES, JEWELLERY AND CERAMICS

GUILFORD HOUSE

Very attractive showroom filled with authentic antiques.
✉ 63 Guilford Street
☎ (26610) 476398

KALTSAS

This fine jeweller is popular with locals and visitors alike and offers stylish designs and top brand watches.
✉ 28 N Theotoki Street/41 Evgeniou Voulgareos Street
☎ (26610) 23830/1

MINISTRY OF CULTURE MUSEUM SHOP

Just inside the entrance archway to the Old Fortress, this bookshop and gallery sells seriously expensive art and archaeological replicas.
✉ Old Fortress ☎ (26610) 46919

MOHAMED KORIEM CERAMICS

Attractive ceramic ware and other craftwork.
✉ 56 Guildford (Town Hall Square) ☎ (26610) 45610

OLIVE WOOD WORKSHOP

Carved wooden objects, both decorative and functional. You'll find imaginative designs, large and small. Good gifts to take home.
✉ 27 Filarmonikis 54 G Theotoki ☎ (26610) 40621

TERRACOTTA

In the heart of the Campiello, the old part of Corfu Town, this stylish shop has a good selection of jewellery, ceramics and sculptures and specialises in contemporary Greek art and crafts.
✉ 2 Filarmonikis ☎ (26610) 45260

THEOFANIS SP. LYKISSAS

Replica icons, candles and ecclesiastical objects.

✉ 18 St Spyridon's Square (Plateia Iroon Kypriakou Agonos)

☎ (26610) 47397

FOOD AND DRINK

ANDRIOTIS

Traditional confectionery such as *mandoláto* (almond nougat), *mandoles* (burnt sugared almonds) and walnut chocolate, as well as bottles of Kumquat (► 78) in the shape of Corfu.

✉ Arlioti Maniarizi 1

☎ (26610) 38045

COSTAS THIMIS

Terrific selection of wines, spirits and liqueurs.

✉ N Theotoki

☎ (26610) 44070

KRITICOS

Irresistible selection of sweets to ruin any holiday diet. Charming service.

✉ Town Hall Square

☎ (26610) 40444 ✉ G Theotoki ☎ (26610) 26676

MARCOS MARGOSSIAN

This wonderful coffee, wine and spirit shop also sells sweets and biscuits.

✉ 20 G Theotoki Avenue, (south side, opposite Pallas Cinema)

NOSTOS

Tasty cakes, pastries and desserts. Wines and spirits.

✉ St Spyridon's Square (Plateia Iroon Kypriakou Agonos). On approach to Church of St Spyridon

☎ (26610) 47714

STARENIO

Traditional bread, honey cake and sweet biscuits with numerous delicious flavours.

✉ Guilford ☎ (26610) 47370

MARKET AND MAIN SHOPPING AREAS

FRUIT AND VEGETABLE MARKET

Corfu Town's lively morning market beneath the walls of the New Fortress has an excellent selection of vegetables, fruit and all types of olives. Fresh fish is also sold and few stalls of clothes and souvenirs.

✉ G Markora 🕐 Mon–Sat 7–1.30

G THEOTOKI/ VOULGAREOS

A range of shops.

✉ Main linking streets that run northeast from San Rocco Square to the Old Town

MITROPOLITI METHODIOU

Middle-market clothes, shoe and hardware shops.

✉ Street running southwest from San Rocco Square

N THEOTOKI

Numerous fashion shops, jewellers, wines and spirits.

✉ Runs from behind the Liston towards the New Fortress

SEVASTIANOU STREET

Great selection of stylish fashion and shoe shops.

✉ Runs from behind the Liston to M Theotoki Street

XENOFONDOS STRATIGOU

Ships' chandlers and hardware shops.

✉ Main road running west between the Old and the New Port

NEWSPAPERS AND MAGAZINES

Most daily newspapers from Britain and Northern Europe are on sale in Corfu the day after publication. Weekly digests of some dailies are also available. Magazines of all types are on sale in the famous Kiosk (► 75) and in newsagents and *peripteros* (kiosks). An excellent English-language newspaper is *The Corfiot*, published monthly. It contains news and features on island life and some very useful listings and advertisements.

'ADULT' SOUVENIRS

In Greece, many tourist-orientated shops do not distinguish between 'adult' souvenirs and those suitable for anyone: you are quite likely to find pornographic books, playing cards, videos etc stacked right next to confectionery or the cash till, rather than discreetly out of sight or on a top shelf. This is something to bear in mind when shopping with children in tow.

Around the Island

Apart from food stores, most shops in resorts close from November to March.

KUMQUAT

This is a famous Corfiot liqueur. It is distilled from the tiny kumquat, a citrus fruit that looks like a miniature orange. It is native to South East Asia and was introduced to Corfu in the 1860s. The standard kumquat drink is bright orange, the colour being derived from the rind; it is very sweet. There is a colourless distillation of Kumquat juice which is far more potent and adventurous and can be identified by the 'twig' with attached crystals that floats inside the bottle. All manner of other drinks, candies and sweets are produced using kumquats.

ACHARÁVI

DALA'S GOLD
A very smart gold- and silver-jewellery shop with various designer wear.
✉ Main street, near west end of resort ☎ (26630) 63684

ELEA
'Elea' in Greek means olive tree, and everything here, including the shop itself, is made of olive wood.
✉ Main street, in centre

AFIÓNAS

KIR ART
This fascinating gallery and work shop is located just as you approach Ágios Geórgios from Afiónas. Artwork covers stainless steel and olive wood, paintings and collages.
✉ Afiónas ☎ (26630) 51925; www.kirart.de

GASTOÚRI

DISTILLERY VASSILAKIS
Unmissable. You will be 'spirited' inside before you are half in or out of the Achilleion gates opposite. Vassilakis has a huge selection of wines, spirits and liqueurs, as well as numerous Kumquat products.
✉ Opposite the Achilleion ☎ (26610) 52440

KASSIÓPI

AGATHA'S LACE
Good selection of handmade lace goods and rugs on offer.
✉ Main Street ☎ (26630) 81315

LÁKONES

THE GOLDEN FOX
As well as accommodation and a restaurant, there is a shop here with local crafts, including rugs, lace, linen and hand-carved olive-wood objects.
✉ Lakones ☎ (26630) 49101

MAKRÁDES

The village of Makrádes (► 55) has become famous for its roadside stalls selling souvenirs, embroidered table linen, knitwear, ceramics, carpets, lace and a range of other goods. A lot of noisy touting and brash sales talk – the experience is part of the deal.
✉ Main road, 35km northwest of Corfu Town

OTHER OUTLETS

AGRICULTURAL COOPERATIVE OF NÝMFES
Kumquat production can be seen at this workshop where there is also a shop. Phone ahead for times of morning openings,
✉ Nýmfes, near Róda ☎ (26630) 94073

KERKYRAIKI ALLANTOPOIIA
Great selection of cured meats and other delacies at this family-run business located just outside Corfu Town.
✉ Paleokastritsa Road ☎ (26610) 91456

Music and Nightlife in Corfu Town

BARS

CAVALIERI HOTEL ROOF GARDEN

The candlelit roof terrace overlooking the town and bay provides the perfect spot for an evening cocktail or light meal.
✉ 4 Kapodistriou Street
☎ (26610) 39041 ⏱ In season 6.30pm–1am

MAGNET

A great place for relaxing over drinks or coffee to a background of mainstream, rock and Greek music.
✉ 102 Kapodistriou Street
☎ (26610) 45295
⏱ 6pm–1am

MOBILE

Modern Greek music at a friendly venue. Price of drinks is above average.
✉ 52 Eth Antistasseos Street
☎ (26610) 34198 ⏱ From midday onwards

MORRISON CAFÉ

Located atop the New Fortress, the unique style of this popular venue is enhanced with some fine jazz as well as rock and pop.
✉ New Fortress ☎ (26610) 27477 ⏱ 6pm–early hours

SAX

The in-place for Corfu Town's younger set, with bright, stylish décor and rocking sounds. Special party nights get going after midnight.
✉ Sebastianou Street
⏱ Evening to late

CINEMAS

Greek cinemas show all the mainstream American and European films. English-language films, are subtitled in Greek and the sound quality is usually good. There is a frustrating, though amusing tendency to interrupt films at reel breaks, often at critical moments of tension, so that everyone can rush to the foyer for snacks and frantic smoking.

ORFEUS

Smaller, more intimate venue with good films, usually in English with Greek subtitles.
✉ Corner of Akadimias Street and Aspioti Street ☎ (26610) 39768/9

PHOENIX

This open-air cinema that only opens during high summer shows Greek and foreign films.
✉ Akadimias Street
☎ (26610) 37428
⏱ Jun–Aug

CONCERTS

OLD FORTRESS

Open-air sound and light extravaganzas in the Old Fortress during the summer. Performances are in English, Greek, French and Italian. There are also performances of traditional folk dance.
✉ Old Fortress, Esplanade
☎ (26610) 48310/48311
⏱ Evening performance

THE ESPLANADE

During the summer months there are musical performances at the bandstand on the Esplanade.

STAYING LEGAL

It is neither polite nor wise to make discourteous public comments about the Greek religion, culture or the State. Such action may be judged as an offence and treated as such by the police.

Recreational drug use, and especially supplying drugs of any kind, is considered a major crime. Supplying even small amounts of drugs may result in a very long sentence of up to life imprisonment. In the event of arrest for any matter, you have the right to contact your consulate.

PHILHARMONIC SOCIETIES

There are 18 marching bands, or Philharmonic Societies, on Corfu. The Corfu Town bands include the oldest, founded in 1840 as the St Spyrídon Philharmonic. The band, whose members wear red uniforms, became known later as the 'Old' Philharmonic after the founding of another society in 1890, the Mantzaros Philharmonic or 'New' Philharmonic, which has a blue uniform. Another Philharmonic Society is the Kapodistrias Philharmonic Union, founded in 1980. The bands and their stirring classical music are an unforgettable part of Corfu's religious and cultural festivals.

CLASSICAL AND TRADITIONAL

Corfu's strong musical tradition is also maintained by the Corfu Symphony Orchestra and Choir, while the students of the Music Department of the Ionian University often perform traditional Greek music in public. The bandstand at the south end of the Esplanade is often the venue for concerts by the Philharmonic Societies and other performers.

THEATRE

MUNICIPAL THEATRE OF CORFU

Fairly regular performances by groups such as Corfu's Municipal Choir. Musical events, opera, drama and dance. There is a licensed bar.
✉ 68 G Theotoki ☎ (26610) 37520

DANCE CLUBS

Corfu has many dance clubs and music bars and all play contemporary styles of music. The dance clubs and music bars of Corfu Town are concentrated at the demurely named Entertainment Centre, better known as 'The Disco Strip', a few kilometres west of the New Port on Ethnikis Antistasseos, the main road from the town to the north and west. The road is very busy with traffic late into the night. When travelling to and from the clubs it is safer to do so by taxi or bus rather than on foot. The average price for a drink is about €5. There is an admission charge at some clubs.

APERITTO

Easygoing music bar with a mix of modern Greek and international sounds.
✉ 40 Ethnikis Antistasseos ☎ (69773) 02566 ⏰ From evening to late

AU BAR

A long-established dance club with a garden cocktail bar and good music. Go late to see it in full swing. Pricey drinks.
✉ 30 Eth Antistasseos Street ☎ (26610) 34477 ⏰ From midnight onwards

EKATI MUSIC HALL

Known for its *bouzouki* band, the Ekati is a stylish, expensive and very Greek nightclub on the edge of town. Large bar, dancing hall; dinners are available.
✉ Alikes Potomós Street ☎ (26610) 45920 ⏰ Daily midnight to late, winter Fri and Sat only

ELECTRON

Electron offers an interesting mix of Greek and European dance music in a tropical ambience. Price of drinks is above average.
✉ Eth Antistasseos Street ☎ (26610) 26793

HIPPODROME

The club with the pool. Big venue catering for 2,000 clubbers. There is a mix of connecting levels, both indoors and outdoors with exotic palms and bar-top dancers. The venue is open in the mornings for coffee, food, drinks and swimming. Price of drinks is above average. The entrance fee includes one drink.
✉ 52 Eth Antistasseos Street ☎ (26610) 43150 ⏰ 11pm onwards

PRIVELEGE

This mainstream, but cool, venue has lots of white landscape and a fairly fashionable clientele.
✉ 42 Ethnikis Antistasseos ☎ (26610) 80780 ⏰ 11pm onwards

Around the Island

DANCE VENUES AND BARS

Resorts such as Kávos, Benítses, Kassiópi and Ipsos are known for late-night dance club action. Most of the popular resorts have clubs and music bars. Bars often aim for the atmosphere of British pubs, many have satellite television and videos on big screens. You will find that clubs will change hands from season to season.

ACHARÁVI

SCARAVAIO
Popular dance club in the main street. Looks like a wooden stockade from the outside. Inside there is a dance area, outside there is a large cocktail bar and floodlit palm trees. Admission is free after midnight.
✉ Main road, by roundabout where road to Episkepsi turns off
☎ (26630) 64455

BENÍTSES

A range of music bars and clubs, all offering much the same in music and a fairly frantic atmosphere. Includes Alcoholics Anonymous, Alexanders, Cheers bar and Casanova's.

DASIÁ (DASSIÁ)

EDEM COCKTAIL BAR
Lasers and videos at this beachside venue and all-night music and dancing. Price of drinks is average.
✉ On Dassiá beach
☎ (26610) 93013
🕐 10.30am–late

GLYFÁDA (GLIFIDA)

ALOHA BEACH CLUB
All-day venue with dance music. Restaurant offering breakfast, lunch and *mezes* in the evening. Wine from the barrel. Price of drinks is above average.
✉ By entrance to beach
☎ (26610) 94380 🕐 10am until late

IPSOS (ÝPOS)/PYRGI

Still fairly devoted to late-night fun and games, typical venues include Bar 52, Hector's, the Temple Bar, Monaco Disco and Dirty Nellies.

KASSIÓPI

Big choice of clubs and music bars including Harbour, Temple, Axis and Angelos.

PALAIOKASTRÍSTA (PALEOKASTRITSA)

LA GROTTA
A great café-bar located in a delightful rocky cove and with a veranda overlooking the sea. It's reached down steps opposite the Hotel Paleokastritsa. Swimming is definitely an option.
✉ Paleokastritsa ☎ (26630) 41006 🕐 All day

SIDÁRI

Discos and dance clubs include Mint and Caesar's. The Palazzo Bar, in the centre, has good cocktails and beers and main street Mikey's Bar is a cheerful venue.

GAMBLING

The island's only casino, at the Corfu Holiday Palace, offers the usual facilities, including roulette. It is open to non-residents. A strict dress code applies and a passport is required for entrance.
✉ 2 Nafsisikas, Kanóni
☎ (26610) 46941/2
🕐 All year

Excellent
Night
Greek dancing

81

Sport, Watersports & Outdoor Activities

CRICKET

Corfu's unique cricketing tradition is a legacy of the British Protectorate. For nearly 50 years the Victorian British garrison played cricket and hosted matches with visiting British Naval personnel. The game was embraced by the Corfiots and for many years the chalked impression of wickets and bails marked many an end wall in the squares of the Old Town where local youngsters played. Today, cricket on Corfu is an essential part of the summer scene on the Esplanade – or has been until recently. The pitch is currently closed and it is not yet known whether it will be restored. A touch rough and ready, it has produced a skilled breed of Corfiot fielders. Visiting clubs from England play regularly on the island, and the Corfu team has represented Greece in European Cup games.

DIVING AND THE LAW

The Greek authorities are extremely sensitive about security at military installations on the island. The use of underwater cameras is forbidden by law unless prior permission is obtained from port authorities. Divers are strongly advised not to dive in working harbours or at busy anchorages.

BASKETBALL

Basketball is now almost as much of a national sport as football in Greece. On Corfu, in every resort, there will be some form of basketball practice area. There are basketball courts at the New Port in Corfu Town, where games can be watched.

CRICKET

Cricket is a famous legacy of the Victorian British Protectorate. Matches are traditionally played on summer afternoons at the north end of the Esplanade, in front of the Liston (► panel, this page).

KERKYRA CRICKET COMMITTEE
☎ (26610) 41205

CYCLING

For information on cycling and mountain-biking (► 20–21).

MORAÏTIKA BIKE HIRE
Rentals to suit all the family.
✉ At southern exit of Moraïtika

THE MOUNTAIN BIKE SHOP
Rentals, cycling trips and holidays arranged.
✉ Main street, Dassiá
☎ Summer (26610) 93344.
Branch also at Grecotel Dafnila Bay Thalosso Hotel, Dassiá

MOUNTAIN MANIA BIKE HIRE
Same management as Yellow Boat Company, which arranges boat hire and excursions.
✉ Main street south, Sidári
☎ (26630) 95555

DIVING

There are outstanding diving venues in the clear waters round Corfu's coasts. Contact a local diving club or school for safety information (► panel this page for regulations).

CALYPSO DIVING CENTRE
The centre is located right on the beach
✉ Ágios Górdis ☎ (26610) 53101; www.divingcorfu.com

CORFU DIVERS
P.A.D.I. teaching centre offering openwater boat diving and all types of dives with instruction.
✉ Kassiópi ☎ (26630) 29226; www.corfudivers.com

CORCYRA DIVING CENTRE
Runs boat trips to numerous excellent diving sites, for beginners to advanced. Lessons available for all abilities. Arranges specialist night dives and cave exploration.
✉ Paleokastritsa ☎ (26630) 41604; www.corfuscubsdiving.com

GOLF
CORFU GOLF CLUB
Corfu's only golf club has an 18-hole course in pleasant surroundings, with a winding river to add to the challenge. Putting green, practice area and club professional.
✉ Rópa Valley, Ermones
☎ (26610) 94220
💷 Expensive

HORSE RIDING
Horse riding is a pleasant and relaxed way of

discovering the quieter side of Corfu. Riding stables offer organised rides. The horses and ponies are well-trained and docile. Children who are capable of riding are catered for.

RÓPA VALLEY RIDING STABLES

Horse and pony riding for the beginner and the experienced rider.
✉ Érmones ☎ (26610) 94220 💰 Moderate

TENNIS

Several luxury and A-class hotels have their own tennis courts which may be available to non-residents by arrangement.

CORFU TENNIS CLUB

The club has four hard courts in a pleasant setting in Corfu Town.
✉ 4 Romanou Street/Vraila Street, Corfu Town ☎ (26610) 37021 🕐 The courts are available to non-members from 8AM to midday

WATERSPORTS

Most of the main resorts and several much smaller beach areas offer watersport facilities from pedaloes and canoes to banana boats, ringos, jet-ski trips and paragliding. Rental outfits operate from most beaches and beachside hotels have hire outlets and supervised watersport facilities which are usually available to non-residents.

SAILING

The Ionian Sea is one of the most amenable areas of the Mediterranean for sailors. There are marvellous cruising opportunities between islands and summer conditions are usually favourable, without the fierce winds of the Aegean. There are a number of sailing clubs based on Corfu itself and there are several yacht chartering agencies. Experienced sailors can charter a yacht themselves or you can book a cruise with an experienced skipper. The Gouviá Marina has very good berthing facilities for those with their own vessels.

GOUVIÁ MARINA
☎ (26610) 91475/91376

CORFU YACHTING
✉ 12 Dorpfeld Street ☎ (26610) 32273; www.corfuyachting.com

WINDSURFING

Windsurfing is an increasingly popular pastime on the breezier beaches of the west coast and at some suitable east coast resorts. These are good waters to learn on, to have fun on, or to enjoy speed sailing on, though there is not much scope for full-on wave jumping.

There are windsurfing centres at the following resorts:
Ágios Geórgios (Northwest), Ágios Geórgios (Southwest), Ágios Górdis, Ágios Stéfanos (Northwest), Arillas, Avláki Beach, Érmones, Glyfáda, Kávos, Moraïtika and Sidári.

NUDE BATHING

Officially, nude bathing is illegal in Greece, although some beaches are now designated officially as 'naturist'. Bathing nude 'unofficially' is best done with discretion. The Corfiots are broadminded but many will be offended by full nudity, especially near centres of population or within sight of a church. Topless bathing by women is virtually the norm on all beaches, but you should respect the sensibilities of local people when off the beach and near religious institutions.

GENERAL PHOTOGRAPHY

Photographs are among the best things to take home from Corfu and the opportunities for all types of photography are limitless. However, near military installations, and at other sensitive sites on Corfu, notices indicating that photography is forbidden should be heeded, or you may find yourself surrounded. In churches, monasteries and museums check first whether or not photography is permitted.

CORFU
practical matters

BEFORE YOU GO

WHAT YOU NEED

● Required — Some countries require a passport to remain valid for a minimum
○ Suggested — period (usually at least six months) beyond the date of entry –
▲ Not required — contact their consulate or embassy or your travel agent for details.

	UK	Germany	USA	Netherlands	Spain
Passport/National Identity Card	●	●	●	●	●
Visa (regulations can change – check before you travel)	▲	▲	▲	▲	▲
Onward or Return Ticket	▲	▲	▲	▲	▲
Health Inoculations (tetanus and polio)	○	○	○	○	○
Health Documentation (reciprocal agreement: ➤ 90, Health)	●	●	▲	●	●
Travel Insurance	●	●	●	●	●
Driving Licence (National or International)	●	●	●	●	●
Car Insurance Certificate (if own car)	●	●	●	●	●
Car Registration Document (if own car)	●	●	●	●	

WHEN TO GO

Corfu

High season

Low season

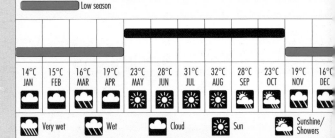

14°C JAN	15°C FEB	16°C MAR	19°C APR	23°C MAY	28°C JUN	31°C JUL	32°C AUG	28°C SEP	23°C OCT	19°C NOV	16°C DEC

☔ Very wet   ☁ Wet   ☁ Cloud   ☀ Sun   ⛅ Sunshine/Showers

TIME DIFFERENCES

GMT	Corfu	Germany	USA (NY)	Netherlands	Spain
12 noon	2PM	1PM	7AM	1PM	1PM

TOURIST OFFICES

In the UK
Greek National Tourist
Organisation (GNTO)
4 Conduit Street
London, W1S 2DJ
☎ 020 7495 9300
Fax: 020 7287 1369
www.gnto.gr

In the USA
Greek National Tourist
Organisation (GNTO)
645 Fifth Avenue
New York, NY10022
☎ 212/421 5777
Fax: 212/826 6940
www.greektourism.com

ARRIVING

Charter flights from European capitals go direct to Corfu in season. Olympic Airways and Aegean Airlines operate flights daily from Athens to Corfu. Ferries run to Corfu from Bari, Brindisi, Trieste and Venice in Italy. Ferries run between Igoumenitsa on mainland Greece and Corfu. KTEL buses run twice daily between Athens and Corfu.

Corfu Airport
Kilometres to Corfu Town

2 kilometres

Journey times

🚆 N/A
🚌 N/A
🚗 10 minutes

New Port Ferry Terminal
Kilometres to Corfu Town

1.5 kilometres

Journey times

🚆 N/A
🚌 N/A
🚗 5 minutes

MONEY

On January 1, 2002, Greece adopted the euro and the Greek drachma was withdrawn. Euro notes come in denominations of 500, 200, 100, 50, 20, 10 and 5; coins in denominations of 2 and 1 euros, 50, 20, 10, 5, 2 and one cents. Foreign currencies and travellers' cheques can be exchanged at banks, bureaux de change and travel agents. Visa, MasterCard and Eurocard are widely accepted in the main resorts and can be used to take out cash from ATM machines at most banks.

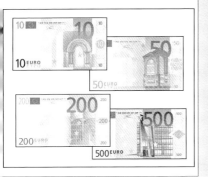

TIME

Corfu, like the rest of Greece, is 2 hours ahead of British time. Greece puts its clocks forward 1 hour in summertime, around the same time as they change in Britain.

CUSTOMS

YES

From another EU country for personal use (guidelines)
800 cigarettes
200 cigars
1 kilogram of tobacco
10 litres of spirits (over 22%)
20 litres of aperitifs
90 litres of wine, of which 60 litres can be sparkling wine
110 litres of beer

From a non-EU country for your personal use, the allowances are:
200 cigarettes OR
50 cigars OR
250 grams of tobacco
1 litre of spirits (over 22 %)
2 litres of intermediary products (eg sherry) and sparkling wine
2 litres of still wine
50 grams of perfume
0.25 litres of eau de toilette
The value limit for goods is €240

Travellers under 17 years of age are not entitled to the tobacco and alcohol allowances.

NO

Drugs, firearms, ammunition, offensive weapons, obscene material, unlicensed animals.

CONSULATES

UK
☎ (2661) 30055 & 23457

Germany
☎ (2661) 31453

USA
☎ (210) 721 2951 (Athens)

Netherlands
☎ (2661) 39900

TOURIST OFFICES

Ellinikos Organismos Tourismou (EOT), the Greek National Tourist Organisation has closed its Corfu Town office and currently (2004) has an office outside town on Eth Antistasseos. There is very little information available at this office. Tourism information kiosks may be opened at locations in Corfu Town for the summer season (2004) but details were not confirmed at the time of writing. EOT website: www.gnto.gr

The Tourist Police should be contacted if visitors have difficulties with, or complaints about accommodation or service.

There are a number of private tourist agencies in Corfu Town that may have some tourism information. They can also arrange accommodation, tours and other services, for a fee. Most resorts have at least one private tourist agency.
A reliable and friendly agency in Corfu Town is:
All Ways Travel
34 G Theotoki Square (San Rocco Square)
☎ (26610) 33955; fax: (26610) 30471; www.corfuallways travel.com

Leaflets on places of interest, car rentals and excursions can often be found at the reception desks of larger hotels.

EMAIL & INTERNET

Corfu Town has several internet cafés including:

Netoikos ✉ 14 Kaloxairetou, (behind The Liston) ☎ (26610) 28637

Café Online ✉ 28 Kapodistriou (just up from Arcadion Hotel) ☎ (26610) 46226

Larger resorts also have internet cafés, usually open until midnight or 1AM.

ELECTRICITY

The power supply in Greece is 220 volts AC, 50 Hz.

Sockets accept two-round-pin continental-style plugs. Visitors from the UK require a plug adaptor and US visitors will need a transformer for appliances operating on 100–120 volts.

NATIONAL HOLIDAYS

J	F	M	A	M	J	J	A	S	O	N	D
2	(1)	1(2)	(1)	1	1		1		1		2

1 Jan	New Year's Day
6 Jan	Epiphany
End Feb/early Mar	Clean Monday
25 March	Independence Day
Mar/Apr	Good Friday and Easter
May 1	Labour Day
June 3	Holy Spirit Day
Aug 15	Feast of the Assumption
Oct 28	Óchi Day
25 Dec	Christmas Day
26 Dec	St Stephen's Day

August 11, the Feast of St Spyridon, is an unofficial public holiday on Corfu. Shops and some restaurants close on public holidays. In Corfu Town and in main resorts, tavernas and most shops stay open.

OPENING HOURS

○ Shops	● Post Offices
● Offices	● Museums
● Banks	● Pharmacies

9 AM	10 AM	11 AM	12 PM	1 PM	2 PM	3 PM	4 PM	5 PM	6 PM
9.30	10.30	11.30	12.30	1.30	2.30	3.30	4.30	5.30	

In addition to the times in the chart above (which are given as a guide only), supermarkets and gift shops, particularly in resorts, often stay open until 9 or 10PM. Pharmacies are closed on Saturday and Sunday. Corfu Town post office is on Alexandras Avenue and opens Mon–Fri 7.30am–8pm. Exchange bureaux are open until 10pm. It is always advisable to check the opening times of museums and sites locally as these vary from summer to winter.

TIPS/GRATUITIES

Yes ✓   No ✗

Restaurants (service included)	✓	change
Cafés/bars (if service not included)	✓	10%
Taxis	✓	change
Tour guides	✓	discretionary
Porters	✓	€1–€2
Chambermaids	✓	discretionary
Hairdressers	✓	10%
Restroom attendants	✓	30 cents
Toilets	✗	

PUBLIC TRANSPORT

 Internal Flights Domestic flights are operated by Olympic Airways (☎ 020 7409 3400; www.olympic-airlines.com) and Aegean Airlines (☎ 801 11 20000; www.aegean air.com) and it is possible to make connections from Athens to Corfu. Olympic Airways domestic flight tickets are non-transferable. All Olympic Airways internal flights are non-smoking.

 Island Buses Corfu's rural bus service is run by the national bus company, KTEL (Kratiko Tamio Ellinikon Leoforion). All services start from and return to Corfu Town. Timetables may be subject to change, but reliability is generally assured. Buses can be boarded anywhere along country roads, and tickets are purchased on board. KTEL buses also run between Corfu and Athens. The KTEL terminus in Corfu Town is at the northwest end of Avramiou. For information ☎ (26610) 30627.

 **Ferries** Ferries run between Corfu Town and Igoumenítsa on the mainland at half-hourly intervals in winter, and as frequently as 15-minute intervals in summer. Ferries also run at hourly intervals between Lefkímmi Port on the southern tip of the island and Igoumenítsa.
International ferries run between Bari and Brindisi in Italy and Patras on the Greek mainland, calling at Corfu Town. Ferry connections between Corfu and Paxos are uncertain and should be checked carefully through several agencies. Greek ferries move very quickly in and out of ports; always be ready to disembark as soon as the ramps touch the quay.

 Urban Transport Blue buses operate from San Rocco Square to the suburbs and Gastoúri (Achílleion), Kondokáli, Gouviá, Dassiá, Pérama, Benítses, Pélekas, Kanóni, and central Corfu. Pay on board or, for buses marked *horis eispraktor*, 'without conductor', buy tickets at the kiosk by the San Rocco bus rank.

CAR RENTAL

 Make sure you have Collision Damage Waiver. However, even with CDW you are liable for damage to tyres and undercarriage, so do not drive conventional vehicles off-road. The minimum rental age is from 21 to 25.

TAXIS

 Call radio cabs on (26610) 33811/2. Taxi ranks in Corfu Town are at San Rocco Square, the Esplanade and New Port. Meters should display the fare; if not determine cost beforehand. Double rates apply outside Corfu Town.

CONCESSIONS

Students/Youths An International Student Identity Card (ISIC) can provide travel discounts and substantial reductions on entrance fees to museums and archaeological sites.

Senior Citizens Most museum and archaeological sites have reduced rates for elderly visitors. There are few other concessions but senior citizens can take advantage of the off-season rates in spring and October – ideal times to visit the island.

DRIVING

 Speed limit on national highways: **100kph**

 Speed limit on outside built-up areas: **80kph**

 Speed limit in built-up areas: **50kph**

 Must be worn in front seats and in the rear where fitted. Children under 10 years are not allowed in the front seat.

 Random breath-testing. Never drive under the influence of alcohol.

 Super, unleaded and diesel are all available. There are few petrol stations in rural areas and they tend to be the most expensive. They open daily (morning only) but may close on Sunday. Cash payment is preferred in rural stations. A useful word is *yemitse*: fill.

 It is compulsory to carry a first-aid kit, a fire extinguisher and a warning triangle. Tourists with proof of AA/RAC or similar membership are given free roadside assistance from ELPA, the Greek motoring club. If your vehicle breaks down, dial 104. There are good repair shops in big towns but in rural areas petrol stations can usually find a local mechanic.

PHOTOGRAPHY

 What to photograph: ancient sites (photography is free for hand-held cameras), villages, parades, harbours. Greek people like being photographed, but it is polite to ask. **Where you need permission to photograph:** in some museums and always if using a tripod. Never photograph near military installations. **Where to buy film:** the most popular brands are available in all tourist areas. The sunlight is brilliant in summer and it is a good idea to use a lens filter.

PERSONAL SAFETY

Corfu is a safe island generally, but crime is on the increase, especially in crowded places. Report any problems to the Tourist Police, who can often speak several European languages.

- Leave money and valuables in hotel safe. Carry only what you need and keep it hidden.
- Women travelling alone can expect some minor harassment from *kamaki*, men on the lookout for a sexual encounter. Be firm in your refusal.
- Do not touch stray dogs. If bitten get medical help.

Tourist Police assistance:
☎ **(26610) 30265**
from any call box

TELEPHONES

The new 10-digit telephone system in Greece now means that for all calls within the country, whether local or long distance, the area code must be used. Furthermore a 2 replaces the 0 at the beginning of the area code, hence what was (06610) 45678 is now (26610) 45678. Phone boxes take OTE phonecards, available from local shops and kiosks, and are the cheapest way to make international calls.

International Dialling Codes

From Corfu to:	
UK:	00 44
Germany:	00 49
USA:	00 1

POST

Post Offices
Post offices have a yellow 'ELPA' sign. Queues can be long and slow and if you only want stamps (*ghramatósima*) for postcards, try kiosks or shops selling cards. Normal post boxes are yellow, express boxes are red. Post offices throughout Greece are generally open Monday to Friday 8–2.

HEALTH

 Medical Treatment
Visitors from the European Union (EU) are entitled to reciprocal state medical care in Greece and should take with them a form E111 available from post offices. However, this covers treatment in only the most basic of hospitals and private medical insurance is advisable.

 Dental Services
Dental treatment must be paid for by all visitors. Hotels can normally provide names of local English-speaking dentists; alternatively ask the Tourist Police. Private medical insurance is strongly advisable to cover dental treatment.

 Sun Advice
Corfu enjoys sunshine for most of the year, and from May until September it is almost constant. During these months, when the sun is at its hottest, a hat, strong-protection suncream and plenty of water are recommended. Try to keep out of the midday sun.

 Drugs
Pharmacies (*farmakio*), indicated by a green cross sign, can give advice and prescriptions for common ailments. If you need prescription drugs, take the exact details from home. Most pharmacies have someone who can speak English.

 Safe Water
Tap water is chlorinated and is regarded as safe to drink. Bottled water is cheap to buy and is widely available. Drink plenty of water during hot weather.

LANGUAGE

The official language of Corfu is Greek. Many of the locals speak English, but a few words of Greek can be useful in rural areas where locals may know no English. It is also useful to know the Greek alphabet – particularly for reading street names and road signs. A few useful words and phrases are listed below, with phonetic transliterations and accents to show emphasis. More words and phrases can be found in the AA *Essential Greek Phrase Book*. Because the method of translating Greek place-names has changed recently, some spellings may differ from older ones you find on the island.

hotel	*xenodhohío*	toilet	*twaléta*
room	*dhomátyo*	bath	*bányo*
...single/double	*monó/dhipló*	shower	*doos*
for three people	*ya tría átoma*	hot water	*zestó neró*
can I see it?	*boró na to dho?*	balcony	*balkóni*
breakfast	*proinó*	campsite	*kamping*
guest house	*pansyón*	key	*klidhí*
toilet paper	*charti iyías*	towel	*petséta*

bank	*trápeza*	exchange rate	*isotimía*
exchange office	*ghrafío sinalághmatos*	credit card	*pistotikí kárta*
post office	*tahidhromío*	travellers' cheque	*taxidhyotikí epitayí*
money	*leftá*	passport	*dhiavatíryn*
cash desk	*tamío*	can I pay by...	*boró na pliróso me...*
how much	*póso káni*	cheap/expensive	*ftinós/akrivós*

restaurant	*estiatório*	bread	*psomi*
café	*kafenío*	water	*nero*
menu	*menóo*	wine	*krasi*
lunch	*yévma*	coffee	*kafés*
dinner	*dhípno*	fruit	*fróoto*
dessert	*epidhórpyo*	waitress	*servitóra*
waiter	*garsóni*	tea (black)	*tsái*
the bill	*loghariazmós*		

aeroplane	*aeropláno*	...single/return	*apló/metepistrofís*
airport	*aerodhrómio*	car	*aftokínito*
bus	*leoforío*	taxi	*taxí*
...station	*stathmós*	the road to...	*o dhrómos ya*
...stop	*stási*	no smoking	*mi kapnízondes*
boat	*karávi*	timetable	*dhromolóyo*
...port/harbour	*limáni*	petrol	*venzíni*
ticket	*isitírio*		

yes	*né*	goodbye	*....adío or yásas, yásoo*
no	*óhi*		
please	*parakaló*	sorry	*signómi*
thank you	*efharistó*	how much?	*póso káni?*
hello	*yásas, yásoo*	where is...?	*poú eené..?*
good morning	*kalí méra*	help!	*voíthia!*
good evening	*kalí spéra*	my name is...	*meh léne*
good night	*kalí níkhta*	I don't speak Greek	*then miló helliniká*
I don't understand	*katalavéno*	excuse me	*me sinchorite*

REMEMBER

- The airport departure tax is added to the price of your ticket when you purchase it.
- It is forbidden to export antiquities and works of art found in Greece.
- Allowances for exporting other goods vary with the destination – check before departure.
- Confirm your flight times the day before departure.

Index

TwinPack
Corfu

Written by   Des Hannigan
Designed and produced by AA Publishing
Editorial Management Apostrophe S Limited

A CIP catalogue record for this book is available from the British Library.

ISBN-10: 0 7495 4334 5
ISBN-13: 978 0 7495 4334 1

Material in this book may have appeared in other AA publications.

Published by AA Publishing, a trading name of Automobile Association Developments Limited, whose registered office is Southwood East, Apollo Rise, Farnborough, Hampshire, GU14 0JW. Registered number 1878835.

Colour separation by Keenes, Andover
Printed and bound by Times Publishing Limited, Malaysia

ACKNOWLEDGEMENTS
The pictures in this book are from the Automobile Association's own library (AA WORLD TRAVEL LIBRARY) and were taken by STEVE OUTRAM, with the exception of the following:
STEVE DAY Back Cover cb, 7t, 15, 25b, 28t, 28c, 30t, 30c, 31t, 33t, 34t, 38t, 39t, 39b, 51, 59, 85b; PHILIP ENTICKNAP Front Cover (flowers); TERRY HARRIS Front Cover (cats, sunbather); S & O MATHEWS 90c, 90r; KEN PATERSON Front Cover (coffee), Cover background, 13b, 60; TONY SOUTER 57; JAMES TIMS Front Cover (church), Back Cover ct, 5t, 8, 14, 16, 20c, 21, 23t, 24t, 27, 29, 33c, 40t, 40b, 42b, 43t, 43b, 44t, 48t, 49b, 50, 52; MARTIN TRELAWNEY Front Cover (statue), Back Cover b, 6, 9, 25t, 38b, 44b, 61, 84; PETER WILSON Front Cover (palm tree, salad)

A01922
Cover maps produced from mapping © Freytag-Berndt u. Artaria KG, 1231 Vienna-Austria
Fold out map © Freytag-Berndt u. Artaria KG, 1231 Vienna-Austria

Dear **TwinPack** Traveller

Your comments, opinions and recommendations are very important to us. So please help us to improve our travel guides by taking a few minutes to complete this simple questionnaire.

You do not need a stamp (unless posted outside the UK). If you do not want to cut this page from your guide, then photocopy it or write your answers on a plain sheet of paper.

Send to: **The Editor, AA TwinPack Travel Guides, FREEPOST SCE 4598, Basingstoke RG21 4GY.**

Your recommendations…

We always encourage readers' recommendations for restaurants, nightlife or shopping – if your recommendation is used in the next edition of the guide, we will send you a *FREE* **AA TwinPack Guide** of your choice. Please state below the establishment name, location and your reasons for recommending it.

_____

_____

_____

_____

Please send me **AA TwinPack**

Algarve ☐   Corfu ☐   Costa Blanca ☐   Costa del Sol ☐   Cyprus ☐
Gran Canaria ☐   Lanzarote & Fuerteventura ☐   Madeira ☐
Mallorca ☐   Malta & Gozo ☐   Menorca ☐   Tenerife ☐
(*please tick as appropriate*)

About this guide…

Which title did you buy?
AA *TwinPack* _____
Where did you buy it? _____
When? 🔲 🔲 / 🔲 🔲

Why did you choose an AA *TwinPack* Guide? _____

_____

_____

_____

_____

Did this guide meet your expectations?
Exceeded ☐   Met all ☐   Met most ☐   Fell below ☐
Please give your reasons _____

_____

_____

continued on next page…

Were there any aspects of this guide that you particularly liked? _____

_____

_____

Is there anything we could have done better? _____

_____

_____

About you…

Name (*Mr/Mrs/Ms*) _____

Address _____

_____

_____ Postcode _____

Daytime tel no _____

Please only give us your mobile phone number if you wish to hear from us about other products and services from the AA and partners by text or mms.

Which age group are you in?

Under 25 ☐   25–34 ☐   35–44 ☐   45–54 ☐   55–64 ☐   65+ ☐

How many trips do you make a year?

Less than one ☐   One ☐   Two ☐   Three or more ☐

Are you an AA member? Yes ☐   No ☐

About your trip…

When did you book? m m / y y   When did you travel? m m / y y

How long did you stay? _____

Was it for business or leisure? _____

Did you buy any other travel guides for your trip?

If yes, which ones? _____

Thank you for taking the time to complete this questionnaire. Please send it to us as soon as possible, and remember, you do not need a stamp (*unless posted outside the UK*).

Happy Holidays!

The information we hold about you will be used to provide the products and services requested and for identification, account administration, analysis, and fraud/loss prevention purposes. More details about how that information is used is in our privacy statement, which you'll find under the heading "Personal Information" in our terms and conditions and on our website: www.theAA.com. Copies are also available from us by post, by contacting the Data Protection Manager at AA, Southwood East, Apollo Rise, Farnborough, Hampshire GU14 0JW.

We may want to contact you about other products and services provided by us, or our partners (by mail, telephone) but please tick the box if you DO NOT wish to hear about such products and services from us by mail or telephone. ☐